the elixir within

Awakening Sexual Radiance for a More Vibrant Life

heather leanne chapman

shashi bear books

Copyright © 2025 by Heather Leanne Chapman

All rights reserved.

Published in the United States by Shashi Bear Books, an imprint of Hearth House LLC.

No part of this book may be used or reproduced in any manner whatsoever without the prior written permission of the publisher and the copyright owner.

No AI training.

The stories that appear in this book are based on real experiences. Some of the stories are composites. For privacy reasons, some names, locations, and dates may have been changed.

The author of this book does not dispense medical advice or prescribe the use of any technique as a form of treatment for physical, emotional, or medical problems without the advice of a physician, either directly or indirectly. The intent of the author is only to offer information of a general nature to help you in your quest for emotional, physical, and spiritual well-being. In the event you use any of the information in this book for yourself, the author and the publisher assume no responsibility for your actions.

ISBN 979-8-9918789-0-6 (paperback)

ISBN 979-8-9918789-1-3 (e-book)

Cover design by Erik Mathiesen

Front cover image copyright © Twins Design Studio / shutterstock.com

www.heatherleannechapman.com

acknowledgments

THANK YOU!

Breanna Chia, Jessica Shoemaker, Pete Hsu,
Tao Semko, Roshi Wendy Egyoku Nakao, Christa Evans,
Renee Palmer, Elisa Schwartz, Ben Loory, Samantha Dunn,
Anna David, Timothy Gager, Azul Terronez, Heather Lee
Dyer, DeeAnn Alongi, Erik Mathiesen, Mom & Dad

AND

Thank you, Spirit. Thank you to my ancestors and my guides.
To my intimate partners who've played and practiced with
me! Thank you to those who've walked this path before
and to all who blaze a trail.

contents

1. THE INVITATION	1
practice: the breath	2
2. MY PUSSY = SUNSHINE	8
practice: connect with your wilderness	11
3. MY BIG SEXUAL REVOLUTION	21
4. AN EGG IN LOVE	27
practice: orbiting (down the spine, up the front)	30
practice: orbiting (up the spine, down the front)	32
5. MOVE IT!	35
practice: feel yourself	37
6. MY EROTIC PROJECT	41
7. YOU CAN TOUCH YOURSELF	49
practice: make love to your hand	50
practice: give your breasts some love	53
8. BE KIND TO YOURSELF	56
practice: ask your wilderness	59
9. CONSECRATION	62
practice: anoint yourself	63
10. RECEIVING PLEASURE	67
practice: the blueberry & the alien	71
11. THE VOICE	78
practice: smile from the back of your brain	79
12. CIRCULATING PLEASURE	81
practice: five gates breathing	82
practice: the breath as your lover	89
13. BUILDING PLEASURE	91
practice: ride the wave	92
14. PERFORMANCE ANXIETY	97
practice: go slow	99

15. S-E-X   102
    practice: the goal is no goal   104

16. YOU ARE ENOUGH   109
    practice: get some sleep   110
    practice: stay in bed   110

17. CLOSING   116
    practice: soap bubbles   121

    About the Author   127

1
the invitation

I'm here to invite you to your very own party. It's just for you. I didn't create this party for you. I'm not sure who did. In fact, I couldn't tell you the first thing about it, because it's yours. It's all for you. It's your party.

All I know is you're meant to go, and it's my job to get you to say yes. I've got to make this invitation irresistible. Your yes must be inevitable. But what can I say that will make you stop what you're doing for half a second and listen? How about this?

Take a breath with me.

Let's just take a deep breath together. In—and out.

There.

You're not entirely happy, are you?

You don't know why.

Maybe you're tired.

Or overwhelmed.

You know you should feel different than you do. You should feel more. You should feel better. You should be happier?

I think I can help. Not that I can make you happy, but then being happy isn't the point. You're going about it all wrong. What you want is to feel *alive*. Lusciously, vibrantly alive.

Am I right?

Is that what you want?

Let's take another breath.

In—and out.

See there?

What was that?

That intake of some sacred invisible elixir without which your life on this planet would end in minutes. You do it all the time. You breathe in, you breathe out. What is that? Yes, yes, you're breathing, but have you ever really thought about it? It's magical! Some kind of interface between you and all that is. Happening over and over until the minute you die.

Let's start here. Let's start with this breathing thing. This magical inhalation.

I'll tell you a secret. This is *the* secret.

You are alive.

And that is something.

That's really something.

We've got a lot of ground to cover, so while this is an introduction of sorts, let's just jump in to:

practice: the breath

Any time you feel lost, take a breath.

In—and out.

This is always here for you.

It's like a train that's always arriving, so whenever you think of it you can hop on.

In. Out.

Oh, hi. You're here.

See, that's how it works.

One more thing.

Let the breath fill you up.

Yes, we all know when we breathe the air goes into our lungs, but just indulge me here and pretend the breath goes all the way to the bottom of your belly. In fact, you can expand your belly all the way out when you breathe, as if you were filling your belly with air. You can breathe into your back too, as if the breath could fill you up in 360 degrees. Breathe down into your pelvis, down into your sexual organs.

Oh! Did I not mention this? I'm very plain when I talk about the body. Graphic even. It's important, so please hang in there with me. It might feel awkward for you, but this thing about the body is key to everything I have to say. So, I can't leave anything out, you see?

Okay, back to the breath.

In.

Out.

Open up the belly.

Expand the breath backwards toward your spine.

Breathe all the way down into your sex organs.

You should be feeling a little more alive right now.

Good.

It may not seem like much, but you've just been initiated into thousands of years of wisdom teachings. You didn't have to fly to Bali or listen to loads of panelists at some symposium on Tantra. This is what they'd tell you anyway. Well, this and more. But we'll get to that.

For now, remember this. The party being constantly created just for you is your life. Your truest, deepest, fullest life. It's right here in front you. And the way in begins with the simplest step.

Take a big belly breath whenever you remember to do it.

In case you're wondering who I am, let me tell you a bit about myself.

I'm Heather. Nine years ago I went on a deep dive into what I call my Big Personal Sexual Revolution. I wrote my blog *How to Come Back to Life* about it. I called it that, because I really did feel dead inside before reconnecting with my sexual energy. I'll tell you more about that as we go along.

Since childhood, I've been a deeply spiritual person, but looking back, I see I've also always been this very sexual creature. What I learned on my journey was the sexual me and the spiritual me are inextricably linked. And—who knew?!—ancient traditions around the world have explored this sacred connection for thousands of years.

In fact, our sexual energy itself is sacred. It's life force energy. That spark that creates life is also the animating force essential to our health and wellbeing. It's the oomph that makes life worth living. It's not that we need to have a roaring fire going inside us all the time, but we do feel our best when that spark is aglow.

You may feel this energy yourself (or dimly remember it) as a constant hum in the background that's always present, a feeling you might not identify as sexual energy, but if you think about it, it does have a subtle sensual quality to it.

In fact, you don't need to be having sex (or even like having sex) to experience that flickering, shimmering energy within you. You can cultivate its flow in your body through sexual practices, but you can also cultivate it through more expansive breathing, paying attention to your five senses, and by consciously feeling the flow of energy through your body.

If none of this makes sense right now, don't worry. You'll start to get a feel for what I mean as we continue. It can be helpful though to think of sexual energy as an essence in itself, like a stockpile of effervescent nectar within you.

I look with so much love on the woman I was nine years ago and the strange disconnect that existed between me and my body. Even though I had a beautiful life, something at the core of it was missing. I was pouring all my creative energy into writing a food blog, and I see now that the pleasure I took from cooking and eating was my only way at that time of having a sensual experience. Some part of me must have known the solution to the deadness I felt inside had to do with being sexually shut down.

I began to pore over sex manuals and instructional YouTube videos, grasping for a life raft in a sea of numbness. I laugh now at some of the crazy shit I tried, because wow, once I was in, I was all in! My friends looked on with hesitant support, gung-ho enthusiasm, or sincere concern as I plunged myself into endless workshops and trainings.

Meanwhile I was gifted with exquisitely subtle, soul-wrenchingly beautiful, volcanic, heart-exploding, and, oh yeah, super-hot sex with myself and with my partners. That numinous energy of life began to course again through the cells of my body. For a long time I thought the gift I'd received was all that great sex. I know now it was also the resurgence of my own vitality.

And now?

I feel there's got to be a way to distill into a simple download all the ancient wisdom I've gleaned so far. I want to share with you how you can access your life force energy and channel it into a more radiant experience of everyday life. I mean, you're here in a physical body on this planet spinning through space. It's wild, isn't it? Don't you want to feel this as fully as you can while you're here? Reading this book, you'll taste what's possible for you—a physical experience of sweetness and warmth—and you'll have a roadmap for how to get back here whenever you want.

When I talk about sexual energy, you may think I'm talking about how to get it on with a partner. While there's plenty of that here, you can't go around having orgasms all day. Also, like I said, sexual energy doesn't always feel sexual. That's why we have words like *libido* and *eros* that convey the larger motions of vitality within us that stem from that deep impulse to procreate *and* spur us to bang on drums and build temples. So, while the practices in this book can lead to way better sex, my main goal is to teach you how to access that vital spark that's inside every human body. How to cultivate pleasure in the simple moments of your daily life. Not just sexual pleasure, but the thrill of being alive in your own skin.

There's nowhere you need to go, nothing you need to do, no partner or guru you need to find to tap into the magic of your life force energy. It's accessible in this very moment. It's who you are. Whether you feel it now or not, that aliveness is right here inside you, waiting to wake up.

I'd like to have told you all the things I learned once I was at the end of my path, seated on some golden throne, gorgeously gleaming with an aura of wisdom all around me. As it turns out, we humans never arrive at that point. Rather than seeing me as some kind of master or expert, think of me instead as your classmate, ahead of you by a few years. I'm just telling you what I'm learning as I experience it, and maybe you're right behind me and I can help you leapfrog through a grade or two. At the very least I can show you my easy way through.

I need you to promise me something. Promise me you'll stay the course. Even if it means dropping off for a day or two, or a couple of months or a few years. Promise me you'll come back to this.

Not to me, but to this.

This endeavor of opening to your own life.

Pinky swear it.

Okay, good. Let's go.

2
my pussy = sunshine

IT'S TIME FOR YOU TO KNOW, YOU ARE PRECIOUS.
YOUR VERY BODY, YOUR FLESH AND BLOOD AND BONES, EVERY INCH OF YOU IS HOLY GROUND.
YES, THAT INCLUDES YOUR PUSSY.
YES, THAT INCLUDES YOUR PENIS, YOUR TESTES, YOUR BUTTHOLE.
EVERY.
SINGLE.
INCH.
SACRED.
PAY NO ATTENTION TO THE MILLENNIA OF SHAMING AND OUTRAGE THAT RISE UP TO TELL YOU DIFFERENT. FACE THAT TIDAL WAVE AND LET IT CRASH OVER YOU. FIND YOU'RE STILL HERE. YOUR PUSSY IS STILL BREATHING, LIFE STILL TWINKLES.
YOU—YES YOU—ARE SACRED.
YOU ARE NOT UGLY OR BAD OR DIRTY.
PLAY AT THAT IF YOU WANT, BUT KNOW DEEP DOWN EVERYTHING ABOUT YOU IS ALRIGHT. EVERY LITTLE THING ABOUT YOU IS JUST RIGHT.
RETURN.
RETURN TO YOURSELF.
YOU ARE HOLY, MY LOVE. HOLY.

IF I COULD PRAY OVER YOU ROCKING TO AND FRO, AS I HOLD YOUR SLANDERED BODY.

MOST HOLY, MOST HOLY.

IF I COULD ROCK YOU TO SLEEP AND LET YOU DREAM OF YOUR OWN RADIANCE.

IF I COULD HELP YOU CONQUER THE SHAME THAT'S SUBJECTED YOU ALL THESE YEARS, I'D TELL YOU:

YOU ARE QUEEN.

YOU ARE KING.

YOU DO NOT KNOW YOUR OWN NATURE. YOU DO NOT KNOW YOUR TRUE VALUE.

YOU MUST WAKE UP.

YOU MUST REMEMBER YOURSELF.

ONLY YOU CAN DO IT.

IT IS TIME, MY LOVE. IT IS TIME.

Are you still breathing?

In. Out. Yes!

Good!

Remember that part where we breathed down into our sex organs? Let's do that again.

Going forward I'm going to call my sex organs *pussy*, because, well, that's what I call mine. And *sex organs* sounds weird. But you can call yours whatever you want based on the bounds of your imagination as well as your anatomy and/or gender. What matters is that this part of your body is where a tremendous amount of untapped power and wisdom resides within you.

Does this idea that your sexual center can be a source of deep inner knowing come as a shock to you? Many of us—especially women—have been conditioned into feeling this part of us is dirty and gross, shameful or even dangerous. It can take decades to unravel that kind of conditioning, and at the moment we don't have that kind of time. So, just for now, we're going to pretend we never learned all that, and we're going to drop down into our sex center / honeypot / lightsaber and see what we feel.

So, here's what I'm doing. I'm taking a deep breath in. And out.

I'm letting the breath reach all the way down into the bowl of my pelvis, and down into my pussy.

She feels pretty awake today.

Hi there! How are you, gorgeous?

I'M GREAT!!!!!

See, that's how it usually goes with her. My pussy can be very loud. Not all the time. Sometimes she's quiet or even withdrawn. But when she's happy, watch out.

What would you like to do right now, Pussy?

TAKE A BREAK!

Okay, then. I guess I'll step away from writing this and take a five-minute dance break. Yes, I'm literally going to dance around my living room for five minutes. And eat something.

YES!!!

Okay, we're back. My pussy knows way more than I do. For example, I lost track of time and didn't realize I hadn't eaten dinner.

Now, you try.

practice: connect with your wilderness

I know this sounds odd, but throughout this book I'm going to refer to your sexual organs as *your wilderness*. Uff, I can already see the memes.

Why use a euphemism rather than just saying *penis* or *vagina*? Well, in that last sentence alone, you must see my dilemma. First of all, some words aren't going to apply to you, so if you identify as a man and you keep reading the word *vulva* over and over, you're going to have to do a mental rewrite every time I use that word. Or if you're a woman and I use the word *vagina*, that might sound too clinical to you. A lot of words could be triggering and make you put this book down and stop reading altogether. And a cute nickname that would be perfect for one person might sound stupid to you. Hence the need for a word that can stand in for all the possible words to describe a person's sexual organs.

Since I'm the one writing this book, I'm going to flex my writerly prerogative and pick a word, and that word is *wilderness*. Why? *Wilderness* captures a lot of the associations I'm going for. It evokes a sense of that seat of power within you, that place of wildness and intensity but also wisdom. Wilderness is a place for both adventure and play, but also where we can experience profound reverence.

I also want to get you thinking beyond individual body parts and aware of the broader ecosystem that is your sexual center. So, we're talking not just your vagina here, but also your ovaries, your uterus, your cervix, vulva, clitoris. We're not just talking about your penis, we're talking about your testes, vas deferens, your prostate. And if you've had something surgically removed—say, your uterus—then we're including the energetic space that remains where that physical organ used to be.

If this word *wilderness* doesn't work for you (and I realize there's a good chance it won't), find your own word and let my use of *wilderness* be your reminder to translate it into your own word. There's no right or wrong here. There's just what feels right for you. You can even play around with different words from one day to the next until you land on one that feels accurate and personal to you. Don't get all in your head about this! Pick a word or a few words that make you smile and start there.

Okay, let's go.

Take a deep breath in and out, letting the breath reach all the way down into your belly, down into your wilderness.

Breathe in and out here for a few breaths.

Down into that wilderness that is you.

What do you feel?

Do you feel anything?

It's okay if you don't. Not feeling anything is a kind of feeling too.

Now, tip your head down a little and look at your wilderness.

If you're alone, I suggest you literally peel back your undies and look down for a second.

Say hi.

Out loud if you want.

Hi there.

Pause.

Give it a minute.

Did you hear anything?

Feel anything?

Sense something?

Again, if not, that's totally fine.

Now ask: *How do you feel?*

You can rest your hand there if that helps you feel more connected.

Breathe another long slow breath down into your wilderness.

And breathe out.

Anything?

Now ask: *What do you want?*

Breathe.

Listen.

———

How was that? Interesting, huh?

I'm going to paint a picture for you now of how absurd it is to feel ashamed of our physical bodies. Imagine you're watching the sun rise, and you turn to me and exclaim how brilliant it is. I respond, "Oh no, don't talk about that! That sunrise needs to cover up. Sunrises should not be discussed in polite conversation. That sun is suspicious. I can't tell you why, but trust me, it's filthy. Shining away over there."

This is how it sometimes feels when I tell people I write about sexual energy. Some people get plain weird on me. Their jaw sets and the light goes out of their eyes like I just offered them something rotten to eat.

No one comes right out and says, "That's terrible! What's wrong with you?" Instead they talk about how much people overshare these days or how careful you have to be about online privacy. One person even "joked" they couldn't hug me anymore because I write about masturbation.

It's so interesting and strange—I can get this response from the most socially liberal people, but I've also received glowing support from folks who are deeply religious. So, there you go. When it comes to sex you just don't know where people are at.

The good news is it takes a second now before I grasp that someone's trying to shut me down. There's this moment where I really do feel like I'm talking about a sunrise, and I can't figure out why the other person wants to crawl out of their skin.

Another analogy: I'm telling you about my new pet parakeet, and she's sooooooooo beautiful. She's got this great big personality! That's how I feel now about my *vagina*! That's how I feel about my clitoris, my cervix, my womb. I'm not kidding when I tell you I fell in love with all of myself.

So when someone looks at me sideways when I say the word pussy, I do know why because that's how I was raised too. At the same time, I don't get it anymore.

Were we all cursed at birth? Did an evil fairy wave a wand over each of us declaring: "You will look at what's sacred with the eyes of the profane! You'll fear the force that created you and brought you into this world! You'll be ashamed of who you are at the deepest level of your being!"

The answer to that is no.

There was no fairy. No curse.

Just generations upon generations of our ancestors taught to believe their bodies were bad and then passing that down to each other and finally to us.

To you and to me.

But I'm looking down at my body right now. It's so amazing. It does so much. I mean, seriously. And my pussy? Wow. What is she, if not the greatest mystery of all time?

And that feeling of pleasure that propels all of life?

Come on!

That's miraculous.

So, when I talk to you about my pussy it really is like I'm telling you about sunshine. When I talk about self-pleasuring, I'm telling you how last night the sun slowly melted into the ocean. When I go on and on about sex, I'm describing the night sky and how wow, doesn't it blow your mind how many stars are out there?

I'm not saying I'm without shame. I've been riddled with it my whole life. But I've got a glimpse now of what's on the other side, and that's love. Me loving me. All of us just loving ourselves already.

———

As I said, I'm not some sexual spiritual master with a canon of wisdom to impart to you. I'm probably just ahead of you on this path, so maybe the most helpful thing I can share is my own stories. Here's one of my journal entries:

June 2019
My pussy is coming out of her shell. I didn't even know she had a shell to crawl out of, but it's the only way I can describe the difference I feel in my body now. My pussy is this soft creature coming forward into the light.

She is present.

She's here with me. I feel her as I write these words. I can feel her when I'm driving. Or washing the dishes. Or sitting at my desk at work. When I'm on the phone. Definitely when I meditate.

She's right here.

I was at ease in my body like this when I was little. I didn't distinguish between my pussy and my elbow or my nose.

It was all just me.

Then all that stuff happened that made me disconnect from her and learn to pretend she wasn't there. By the time I realized I was cut off from her it was hard to be aware of her existence at all, let alone feel her. Now I feel her the same way I feel air going in and out through my nose. Or like I taste the juice of a pineapple.

Is this what people mean when they talk about embodiment? Being in.
My.
Body.

I feel lit up and present, like I have agency in the world. I feel myself filling up space. There was a song we sang in grade school:

I'm alive alert awake enthusiastic!
I'm alive alert awake enthusiastic!
I'm alive alert awake.
I'm awake alert alive.
I'm alive alert awake enthusiastic!

That's it. That's how I feel.

It's counterintuitive, but when I connect to my pussy I feel innocent inside my own skin.

I'm returned to that wholeness I felt as a child.

This is a gift. Life is a gift. I don't know what the fuck we're all doing here, but being here is a gift. I do know that much.

One of my most powerful memories is not actually a memory of my own. It's a story my mom told me about myself:

We were at a big gathering, and you were a little girl. You kept flipping up your dress, delighted to give people a peek at your undies, but your grandma flew into a rage, threatening to spank you. Her anger was so out of proportion to the situation, I kept defending you, pleading, "She's just a little girl!"

I've been thinking about this story a lot. My grandma and I became great friends over time, and there are many other, precious memories of her I'd much rather share with you. But I think how joyful I was in that moment, and how confusing it must have been to learn that this part of my body was so bad it must never be seen. Even as a child, I must have sensed that Grandma's anger had nothing to do with my lack of modesty. That kind of ferocity could only be directed at something very bad.

As an adult, I can imagine her reaction might have been due to protectiveness and an effort to keep me safe. But deep down I know it was about the terrible shamefulness of my little human body.

My mom had a white leather Bible with a zipper around the outside. I used to flip through the pictures in it, but the only one I remember is of Adam and Eve being expelled from the Garden of Eden. There was no picture of them basking in the sun, holding hands as they reveled in the garden's bounty. Instead, the image showed them leaving Eden in shame and disgrace, walking into the wind with heads down, their hands over their private parts, a kind of dustiness all around.

So yeah, like everyone I got lots of messages early on that my body was bad and what it felt was *really* bad. My parents did their best to be progressive and evolved, telling me I was beautiful, letting me know my body's instincts were natural. But it's hard to transmit something you don't have yourself. Ideally, that would have been a sense of ease and confidence with my body and eventually with sex. Instead, the larger culture seeped into me through the kids at school, through teachers and TV shows, movies, music, comic books and Sunday School. All of it taught me to hate my body. And as it turned out, hating my body was the same thing as hating myself.

I don't go around thinking I hate myself, but for a long time I really thought my vagina was disgusting. It was ugly, smelly, leaking strange fluids all over the place. Totally unreliable. Not to be counted on to get turned on at the right time or not turned on at the wrong time. Sure, I read that play *The Vagina Monologues*. I even did some exercise where I looked at my vagina in a hand mirror, but these experiences in isolation couldn't erase years of collective consensus telling me that vaginas are gross.

My wariness toward my pussy probably did begin that day that I don't remember, when I was chastised for showing her off.

You may be wondering how I got to be so chummy with my genitals (there's an ugly word for you). A major milestone for me was reading the book *Pussy: A Reclamation* by the marvelous Regena Thomashauer (aka Mama Gena). Mama Gena showed me, as she's shown countless other women, how to truly love my body. She's the one who taught me to listen to my pussy, to talk to her and tell her every day how gorgeous she is.

Mama Gena revealed a larger cultural context for me, relaying ancient myths and traditions that, had I been raised with them, would have taught me to honor this part of my body. In her book, she shares a myth that was celebrated by the ancient Greeks every year in rites known as the Eleusinian Mysteries.

The Greeks had a myth about the goddess Demeter and her daughter Persephone. Maybe you've heard it. It's a story about why we have the four seasons. Demeter was the goddess of agriculture and fertility. Her daughter Persephone was abducted by Hades and taken to the underworld to be his bride. In her grief and rage at the loss of her daughter, Demeter wandered the earth in despair, inconsolable. She withdrew her light from the world, causing mass drought and starvation.

Finally, Demeter's depression lifted, and she demanded that in order for life to resume on Earth, her daughter must be released. The terms of this arrangement were such that Persephone was allowed to return above the ground, but only for six months of the year, bringing the springtime with her.

Okay, so maybe you know that part of the story. But do you know what it was that shocked Demeter out of her endless grief and back into her own power? It was the goddess of mirth, Baubo. Baubo shows up in the story as a bawdy old woman and starts telling Demeter dirty jokes. She then lifts her skirt and flashes her pussy at Demeter. Demeter smiles, and in that instant her debilitating grief is lifted. She is returned to herself, and the cycle of life on earth is set back into motion.

I'll tell you something. Writing this book terrifies me. I'm afraid of how people will respond to it, how you'll respond. I'm scared you'll get that look on your face like I've said something despicable. The thing is, I'm here to bring you back to your life and like I said, this part about loving your *whole* self is crucial to that.

Oh look, I just took a deep breath.

Huh. You know what? Here I am all these years later, a grown woman and I'm showing off my panties again! Writing this book is me flashing my pussy at you! It's time to tap into that exuberant being inside me again—my dress flipped up, shrieking with glee.

3
my big sexual revolution

If I could tell you one thing about myself, I'd tell you this. I was raised by a river. Yes, the river raised me. Oh sure, my parents were active participants, but the river has been here since before I was born. It was here when I was a child playing mermaid in its deep green waters, when I sat as a teenager on the big rock, meditating before I knew what meditation was, contemplating the muddy rapids below. The river will be here long after I die. It's here now, outside the window of my childhood home, rushing and roaring. Today it's green. The color changes from season to season and from day to day, but today it's green. Which is perhaps my favorite color for it to be.

Why am I telling you this?

What does this have to do with anything?

I have no idea, but the river taught me everything I know.

It taught me to meditate.

It taught me how a stone thrown into it generates concentric circles in the water that expand out to infinity, the same way our actions reverberate through time and space in ways we'll never know.

It taught me salamanders love to fuck.

It taught me frogs and fish and, well—everything—dies.

Dreams can come true, and they can die as well.

Every spring there are new baby birds.

In the summer you can plunge into the cold water all in one go, or you can inch your way in minute by minute. Or you can choose not to get in at all. It doesn't matter what you choose.

All that matters is love and friendship.

The river taught me above all else the sparkle of the sun on the water, the feel of the cold on your skin, fir trees tall and swaying far up in the sky, birds chasing each other down in an endless game.

This, this.

This is why we're here.

This is what I'll remember in that brief second before I'm gone.

All this.

The river taught me the only way to truly know it is to acknowledge I am of it. There's no me admiring the river. There's just all this, and I'm one cell in whatever this is.

I've learned to trust the flow of life, no matter what it delivers to me. No matter if it's what I want or what I think I don't want. No matter the agony or the bliss. Even when it makes no sense. So, while it seems bizarre to tell you I was raised by a river, this is what I'm moved to say to you, so I trust it's what needs to be said.

This is how I knew nine years ago to end my partnership of fourteen years. It's how I knew to throw myself headlong at last into the pursuit of ecstasy. It's how I've known to follow my heart when love has arisen within me. Nothing ever goes where I think it will, yet all is perfection, whether I see it at the time or not. This is what I mean when I say I trust life.

There are so many things I could tell you about myself, so many currents we could follow here. But what's most relevant to what we're talking about now is the subterranean current of my sexuality.

Like I told you, I've always been this very sexual creature. I was the kid on the playground urging other kids to climb the poles of the swing-set so we could giggle at the "ticklish feeling" between our legs. Then once I learned to be ashamed of that feeling, I became the fifth grade girl in the bathroom stall at lunchtime masturbating furiously. Let me tell you, I had a hell of a technique.

You'd think this powerful drive of mine would have made me grow up to be a genius in bed. Not the case. Like most everybody, I received no instruction on how to "do" sex. So, as a young woman I surrendered myself to encounters that ranged from transcendent to unfortunate, depending on the abilities of my partners. I brought a lot of spirit to the game but not much skill. Funny thing though. I once confided to a friend that I thought I might be a nymphomaniac (we say *sex addict* now). My wanting could be so overpowering I sometimes felt it might destroy me.

By my late thirties, the idea of me as a sex addict was laughable. I was in a long-term partnership with the love of my life who was also one of my best friends. I had a great job, we lived in a beautiful home, I had everything a person could want, except for sex. My boyfriend and I had become more like affectionate siblings than romantic partners. I knew this was common in long-term partnerships, and believe me, I told myself that all the time. "This is what happens in committed relationships," I'd say. "It sucks, but it's normal!" To this day, when I tell this story, some people shrug and tell me what I experienced is the norm. They imply I was crazy to expect more. Well, anyway, I did make peace with it to the best of my ability. I had a dim recollection of the ravenous hunger that had sometimes been such a torment to me. Maybe I was okay with sacrificing passion for love. It would have been nice to have both, but what was I going to do? I'd found my soulmate. Not everyone finds a love like that. We were lucky.

We really were so very lucky. At the same time, the thought would occur to me, *I've shut down so much, I can barely feel anything below my neck. It's like my whole body's gone numb.* I became obsessed with writing short plays and stories about women who felt frozen, numb, stunted, or dead.

Then a funny thing happened. My body came back to life. Such a surprise, right out of the blue. One day my honey and I were happily chilling on the sofa, the next I was like a dead person resuscitated on an emergency room table. It was not pretty, let me tell you. All those years of submerged wanting were suddenly unleashed. What had been a sweet and tender companionship became torture to me. I was beyond sexually frustrated; I was enraged, on fire, needing to be filled, to be met.

But the bonfire ignited within me had no effect at all on our sex life. Yes, there'd been quite the charge between us a long time ago, but it was just—gone. And it had been gone for a very long time. After confronting this thing we never talked about—the fact we no longer had sex—and then talking about it endlessly, we agreed to leave the stifling comfort of our little bubble.

It's funny, you know? How months of heartbreak can be condensed down into a few words.

We split up.

Thankfully, we remained super close, and to this day he's my closest companion. But finally, I was free. So began what I call My Big Sexual Revolution.

―――

March 2017
I remember now what I was so afraid of all those years ago. I'd completely forgotten this mountain of desire. Unrelenting, unquenchable. What if I can never feed it? What if I'm left with this profound ache I cannot relieve? I couldn't bear it to need this much, to want this much. Where the wanting blows apart the surfaces I think of as me and all I am is want.

January 2018
I come to you with unimaginable hunger. I can't fathom anything that could satisfy it, not sex, nothing.
And yet, you meet me right here. You lie in this field with me, silent, still, and I am no longer alone with it. You are here, in it, with me.

You go straight to it, go deep. And then we're here, wave upon wave pulsing deep under the ocean.
Who would have thought there was no stroke it needed, nothing to set it loose or set it free? Only to be met, heard, known.

Now—after—this peace I feel inside me is profound.
I'm not afraid.
I am still, sacred, expansive, rooted.
For a moment we were one.
I have touched the center. Like touching my foot down on the floor of the ocean, down at the very bottom, all the while the

*water up above spreading out in all directions to the edge of
the sky.
Spread wide in all directions together.
I will not forget this.
It is now known.*

4
an egg in love

You know how you feel when you wake up from a delicious deep sleep? Like honey's been drizzled through your limbs? You feel light and easy, and there's a sparkle about you. Or the way you feel after great sex—where you feel kind of warm and runny? Like you're an egg cooked over-easy? Ideally an egg that's in love.

That's the feeling we're going for.

It's accessible more often than you'd think. All you have to do is cultivate it and remember to reach for it whenever you can.

Hey! Are you hearing this?

I'm talking about the elixir of life here!

No joke.

Wisdom traditions around the world have sought how to access this blissful state and weave it through the fabric of everyday life. They've also studied how to use it to improve health, become more powerful, or even attain enlightenment. Once they figured all that out, a lot of them kept their discoveries secret. But like all great secrets, the way into bliss is in plain sight. It's like when somebody searches for the meaning of life, and once they find it, they go around saying things like, "We're all one!" or "It's just love!" And everybody's eyes glaze over.

Yes, some of this sounds simplistic. Breathe! Love your body! I can see why you might underestimate the power of these practices.

Just do them. See what happens inside you.

I promise you nothing's in these pages for no reason. All of it matters. All of it! These deceptively simple practices together form the container in which a shift can take root in you on a deep level.

Why am I telling you all these ancient secrets? I don't know, because it's crazy they're a secret!? Okay in all honesty they're not secret anymore. At all. There are tons of books and courses and videos out there. Look online for the definition of *kundalini* or *chi* or *prana* or *ruach* or *the radiant holy breath*. Look up Classical Tantra, Tibetan Buddhist Tantra, ancient Egyptian mythology, Paganism, Hermeticism, Qigong, internal alchemy. Look up images of virility gods and fertility goddesses. With all this information at our fingertips, the big mystery to me is how every person on the planet doesn't know how to tap into their life force energy and feel radiantly alive.

You'll notice this book is focused on teachings from the world's eastern hemisphere rather than from the west. There are two reasons for this. Ever since I was a child, I've been drawn to eastern philosophies like Buddhism and Taoism (though I knew nothing until recently of the branch of Taoism that cultivates sexual energy). Also, maybe you've heard of this thing that occurred in Europe called the Spanish Inquisition and the subsequent burning of witches?

While pagan traditions and even early European religious traditions did explore sexual energy, those traditions were violently and effectively stamped out. Today, they don't have the same unbroken teaching lineages or the abundance of literature that survived in places like China, Tibet, and India.

But maybe you don't care about all this history or even about the elixir of life within you. Maybe you just want to get to the part on how to have more amazing sex.

Here's the thing.

The only way to those spectacular succulent experiences you want is from right here, where you are now. It's true! Learning how to be present. How to ride the breath. Learning to circulate pleasure through your body. These skills—once embodied, once you're doing them in your sleep—will suffuse the very nature of your existence. Then when you're making love you'll remember—oh yeah, breathe—and then, Oh. My. God.

Sometimes the less we scrutinize sex the better. At one time I developed a kind of PTSD around climaxing, and the last thing I needed was to obsess about it all the time or try to fix my "issues." The best thing was taking my eye off that ball entirely (for like, a year) until, whoops! Look at that. An orgasm! So, yes, trust you can stop thinking about where this is all going.

Does sex feel like you're trying to melt an iceberg in fifteen minutes flat? If so, there is a solution to that. In addition to giving yourself way more time, it's about being fully in your body 24/7. Enjoying the sensation of air on your skin, the sun on your back, smelling the rain, actually tasting the food in your mouth.

You might be inclined to skip all that, but all *that* makes all the difference. That's when sex starts to feel like part of the flow of life. See, what you want is to be like a simmering pot of water. Then when sex is imminent, you're right there, ready and open. There's no need to crank up the heat; you just allow the bubbles to roll to a boil.

But maybe you're not frozen. Maybe you're the one who wants sex all the damn time. That's its own torture, right? Again, you can learn to sink into all the pleasure that's already present *here* for you, spreading and diffusing that intensity through your whole torso and your arms and legs, not just your wilderness. This will give you relief and at the same time teach you a whole new luminous way of being in the world.

Now, if better sex is your big goal, you are going to need to educate yourself on that one. So yes, more research! No matter how much you think you know about sex, you can always learn more about your own body, your lover's body, the whole geography and physics and psychology of desire. I've listed resources for you on my website heatherleannechapman.com which include some that will blow your mind on all the ways pleasure is possible in the human body.

Back to our pot of water on the stove. We're going to light the flame underneath. We're going to gently open up the body, so pleasure can stream through us effortlessly and with ease. This will unfold as a softening, a soothing, a gentle unwinding in you. Have fun and enjoy!

practice: orbiting (down the spine, up the front)

Touch the tip of your tongue to the roof of your mouth, behind your front teeth. Keep your tongue here throughout this practice.

Take a deep breath in.

As you breathe *out*, ask yourself:

What if a cascade of golden oil was flowing down through the top of my head, down my back, all the way down my legs to my feet?

Mmmm, that would feel pretty good, actually.

I'll give you a minute to conjure that.

Imagine that warm liquid gold dripping down the back of your skull, down your spine, vertebra by vertebra.

Feel it drip down your tailbone, the backs of your thighs and knees and calves.

Now, imagine as it touches the ground it turns into a gold fairy dust at your feet.

As you breathe in, breathe that gold sparkle right up the front of your body, up your legs, through your hips, through your chest and throat, through the middle of your brain in a gentle flow of delicate glitter.

Pause at the top and hold your breath for the briefest second.

Savor this feeling.

As you breathe out again, the glitter condenses back into liquid gold and drizzles back down the back of your skull, your spine, etc.

Play with this cycle for a while.

Go ahead, close your eyes for a couple of minutes and give it a whirl.

Welcome to the Macrocosmic Orbit! This is a fundamental practice of Taoist Inner Alchemy, developed in ancient China and then introduced to a global audience by Mantak Chia starting in the 1980's. It also shows up in Tantric Kriya Yoga and in Buddhist Anuttara Tantra. I've blinged it out a bit for you. The classic way to do it is to visualize your breath (or even just energy) flowing through your body. Gold and glitter help me more palpably feel it, but you can imagine running just about anything that works for you through your body in this same pattern (you might also try water or light).

We just ran the orbit in reverse—*down* the spine and *up* the front. You can run it in the other direction too, *up* the spine and *down* the front, which is also very nice. Let's try that.

practice: orbiting (up the spine, down the front)

Touch the tip of your tongue to the roof of your mouth again.

Keep it there!

Breathe in and imagine there's a bowl of warm oil nestled inside your pelvis.

Take a minute to get a sense of what that would feel like.

As you breathe in, allow the oil from the bowl to rise up your spine (I know, weird, whatever) along your back to the top of your head.

Pause, hold your breath briefly, and savor.

Now, breathe out and feel the oil drizzle down over your face, your throat, over your chest, your belly, back down into the bowl in your pelvis.

Pause for half a second.

Now breathe the oil back up your spine again.

Etc.

There are millions of ways you can play with this. You can do a big loop (The Macrocosmic Orbit), encompassing the whole body like we did the first time. You can do a smaller loop (The Microcosmic Orbit), from pelvis to head like we did the second time. If you want to get technical about it, with a smaller loop the classic starting point is at your perineum (that little spot between your anus and your wilderness).

Up the spine (the way we just did it) is the more activating motion. *Down* the spine is more soothing. All these pathways work just fine. The goal now is simply to feel energy circulating through your body in a continuous loop. So whether that energy runs under the surface of your skin, or it runs through your spine, or straight through the core of your body, or over the outside of your body like big carwash mitts slathering you with soapy water—it's all good! Don't worry about getting it right. Treat it like a game and see if you feel anything.

Keep in mind—there's nothing here for you to *do* exactly. You're just feeling into a stream of energy that's already flowing. You don't need to make the river go. It's already doing its thing, whether you feel it now or not.

Okay. So maybe you felt something while orbiting or maybe it was a big nothing for you, but trust me. Orbiting's one of those things in life worth taking the time to master. It's one of the best ways to get everything flowing and glowing inside you by tapping into that interior wellspring of vitality. It's also a great way to either wake up or smooth out your sexual energy, depending on your situation.

This particular practice can be tricky for some people to get the hang of. I've recorded a free guided audio practice for you at heatherleannechapman.com/theelixirwithin.

November 2017
My experience is moving so fast, and what I feel today I

know I'll no longer feel and possibly won't even remember tomorrow. So I need to write about what's happening.
I tap into a wave of sensation in my body so readily now. All it takes is a touch, the caress of my finger along the line of my nipple, the grip of his hand around my throat, and I'm right here.
In it.
It wasn't like that before. And I wonder what it will be like next. Already there's so much more I didn't even know was possible to feel. Lines of energy radiating out from my pussy to the soles of my feet, to the very centers of the palms of my hands, through the crown of my head. No one ever told me this was a thing you could feel. Breathing in and out the whole time.

5
move it!

I'm going to ask you now to do something super basic. You're not going to want to do it, and you'll probably wonder why I'm going on about the obvious here.

The thing is, I need you to move your body. Just a little bit! A little bit every day if you can. This is crucial for reaping the benefit of everything I'm sharing. If you want to feel more alive in your body you've got to run some energy through it on a regular basis. You need to get your blood flowing, even if it's for ten minutes. Go for a walk, lift some weights, or my personal favorite—dance!

I really do need you to get up and move (we're talking ten, maybe twenty minutes here). If you don't feel like moving, ease into it. Dip a toe in and see what happens. Open the door, step outside, and walk to the end of the block. Or play a low-key song (maybe even an angry song) that's not so raucously happy it's going to irritate you. Sway your hips halfheartedly from side to side. That counts as moving. So does gently bouncing up and down (some people call this "shaking practice"—check it out). Go easy on yourself, but do please move! I have a whole Not Too Happy Playlist I break out when I feel I can't possibly get up off the sofa. You'd be surprised how many times I've gone from reluctant sloucher to undulating goddess in minutes.

Oh yeah, and about that. We have this idea we need to look good or be sexy when we dance. You can do that. Dance however you like. But you can also try dancing like you're a little kid. What if you were five and nobody was watching you? What weird faces would you make? What funny noises? What kind of animal would you imitate? Stomp up and down, bug your eyes out, have a ball. Or pretend you're an entirely different person. How would you dance if you weren't you? Dance ugly! Dance stupid! Dance silly!

Everything I'm sharing here increases the flow of energy through your body. More flow means more sensation, and that's what we want! You also want that sense of aliveness to flow through you in new ways, opening up new pathways for pleasure. That's not going to happen if you're sitting down all day.

One more obvious thing. Go outside. Just go outside! Ohmygod, look at the sky! What's up there? Clouds? Birds? Take a deep breath. Close your eyes and see if you smell anything. If you feel adventurous, take off your shoes. There's *enormous* power available to you at all times simply by opening a window, stepping outside, connecting up with the vital energy (call it what you want—oxygen, sunlight) that's all around us. This energy is inside you too, but there's nothing like looking at a tree or putting your feet on the earth to make you really feel it.

Here's a question I ask myself all the time: *How do I feel in my body right now?* Or rather, my body asks itself the question. It's less a cognitive thought and more a felt inquiry. How's my abdomen feel? Thick? Clear? Are my neck and shoulders tight? Am I gripping with my hip flexors? Am I even breathing at all right now?

This feeling tone, like the reverberation of a bell within me is the baseline my entire experience of life springs from. And I've learned something. What I think of as a good feeling is not necessarily how I want to feel all the time. For example, an ecstatic feeling tone is not sustainable day to day. Neither is a buzzy turned-on feeling tone.

There's a groundedness and a rootedness I reach for now as a starting point to my day. From there I can layer in a feeling of freshness or brightness. Anything, really. Petulant luxury. Dropped-in stillness. Spaciousness. Deep nourishment. But first I have to start where I am.

practice: feel yourself

There's a feeling tone inside your body.

Can you feel it?

See if you can feel it now.

Breathe.

What's the overall feeling in your body?

Is it dull?

Is it bright?

Cacophonous?

Is it hard and condensed?

Or flat?

Heavy?

Is it shiny? Fuzzy and floaty? Strung out? Jacked up? Tight? Loose?

Give yourself time to listen to the sensation of your body.

Wherever you are on the physical map, let yourself be there. It's okay if what you're feeling doesn't feel good.

If there's a part of your body that needs relief, rest your attention there for a second. There's no need to try and change what you're feeling, but here's something that might give you some relief. Imagine if you could dab a pat of butter on or inside that ouchy place in your body. Yeah, go ahead and picture that. Now, imagine that butter starting to melt the way butter melts in a hot pan. It's got some bubbles in it and it's sizzling a little bit and it's running around and cascading through the crevices of your tension.

You could even mimic the Wicked Witch of the West and joke to yourself, "I'm melting, *melting!*" Breathe gently into this area of your body, as the warm melty butter does its thing. No need for dramatic inhales. Just bring breath to this, some smoothness and space.

This simple check-in will shift things in you. You probably won't be able to keep overworking and pushing through all the time, if that's your thing. When you feel yourself digging into that relentless list of things to do, your solar plexus tightening, your whole body gearing itself up for action, can you interrupt yourself within that well-worn path and do something different? Believe me, you won't want to. You'll want to push through to complete whatever's next on the list. But when you feel that contraction kick in, remember to breathe, and melt.

April 2022
My back hurts this morning. It's that twinge that never goes away. Here I sit, urging people to cultivate this luminous feeling state in their bodies. How am I supposed to write

about ecstasy and pleasure when I've got this mini spasm going on? It's humbling as I write this book to constantly reread my own words. Words like, "I'm going for a sustainable elevated state here. I'm upleveling my daily experience into one of perpetual yumminess."

What was I thinking? That's a tall order.
But why not? Why shouldn't I feel good as much of my life as I can?

The irony is this means doing—each and every day—everything I'm telling others to do. Every time I sit down and look at what I've written, it turns into an automatic check-in with myself. How do I feel? No, how do I really feel? It's a grim revelation how often I don't feel good in my body. Even when I'm having a good day, my muscles are tense and hanging on for dear life. I grip my legs like I've got to hold them onto my body by sheer force of will. And that thick feeling in the pit of my stomach? I just push that down.

I have to keep putting on the brakes and slowing myself to a stop. Ugh, I overdid it again; I feel fried again. More and more this habitual state of tension is becoming unacceptable to me. My baseline now must be ease at the very least. Preferably ease and flow.

A lot of the time the way there is to simply slow down. But then I think to myself, That's impossible. I don't have time to slow down.

Annnnnd that's the mindset that got me here in the first place!

I know I'm proposing a lot. We aren't taught this way of being in the world, but we can learn. I'm living proof. One embodied moment really does beget another. I can inch my way into feeling exponentially better starting with how I feel right now. So yeah, my back hurts. Can I soothe that? What tiny adjustment would bring some relief? Oh, yes. Already I feel different. A little more softness, a little less tension. That's better.

6
my erotic project

Here's the thing. For me to tell you my whole story is going to take so long! There are so many people to tell you about. There's my ex who's still one of my best friends—Ex #1. I'll call him "Honey Pie." Then there's Ex #2 who I almost married but who was ejected so completely from my life four years ago it feels like he died. I'll call him "Bye Baby." Then there are all these other people who've entered and exited my life along the way. There are so many people I'm thankful for —friends, family, playmates, lovers, teachers.

But let's jump to early 2017, right after the U.S. presidential election. I can't overstate the impact the political climate in America had on me at that time. As far as I could tell the world had lost its mind. The very culture that taught me to be a good girl and to hate my body was propping up a man who could do absolutely anything and yet do no wrong. All rules were obliterated, and everything was upside down. I do wonder sometimes—would I have gone another way if the world had been different? Here I was, trying to live my life in the middle of all of it. For over a year I'd been reading all these books and watching YouTube gurus on sex and sexuality, trying to learn how to get back into my body. And I was holding myself back . . . why? For who? What on earth was stopping me from doing absolutely whatever I wanted?

Maybe I was waiting for some new love to manifest for me. If so, I was kidding myself. I was fortysomething. I'd experienced the love of a lifetime. No chance of that happening again. Love, for me, was clearly done. It was time for whatever life had in store for me next.

The piece that was missing, the piece I'd been sitting on all these years was this rushing torrent inside my own body. This lush, primal, hidden place. The place that longed for a seat at the table, seeking expression and integration into the entirety of my life. I didn't know it then—I thought I just needed to get laid—but deep down, what I wanted was for all of me to finally be here.

There are secrets within secrets in this story. Someday when we know each other better, when we're older, perhaps I will tell you. I would love to tell you all of it. Basically, I dove into what I now know was an initiation into the ancient secrets of sacred sexuality. I began calling it My Erotic Project once I started writing about it a couple of years later. But at the time, I was just trying stuff out, trying whatever offered itself to me to be experienced. There was an element of abandon in all I did because I had nothing to lose. My life as a normal person was over. The world was going bat shit crazy, and I figured I might as well do whatever I wanted. I threw myself into the study of Neotantra and Taoist sexual Qigong and god knows what all through online courses, in-person workshops, and friendships with a few wonderful men. They say when the student is ready, the teacher appears? In my case, when I was ready, other students showed up and we educated ourselves together.

On the outside I was living an ordinary life. I worked as a personal assistant and house manager, running a large estate for a wealthy older person (everyone asks—no, no one famous). When people asked what I did for a living, I explained I was the butler on *Downton Abbey*. I worked Monday through Friday 9-5. My office overlooked the vast blue expanse of the Pacific Ocean. I had fantastic coworkers. I commuted a minimum of two hours a day on the freeways of Los Angeles and spent almost that entire time on the phone. I had a rich network of friends. I loved my life.

That was the part of my life most people saw, but my private life was this additional kaleidoscopic universe. I'd become intrigued with the idea of polyamory—this deep truth we can love or be attracted to more than one person at a time. Of course we can! It was a revelation to me that explained so much about my own experience as well as what I'd witnessed in the lives of others. Why not structure your life around that, rather than trying to meet all your needs (intellectual, emotional, sexual) through one person?

And so I delighted in the playful and nourishing communion of these sweet friendships of varying sexual and sensual intimacy, all the while considering *myself* to be my own primary partner/significant other.

I was about a year into this solo-poly experiment of mine, when I fell in love again. And I mean, *fell in love*. Who could imagine being gifted with not one but two precious partnerships on this journey of life? Poly went out the window pretty fast. After some months, Bye Baby (my new love) and I ended our connections with other people and embraced a monogamous relationship. We'd become this little world of two anyway, and juggling a bunch of people was challenging for us, both logistically and emotionally.

We adored each other. Our love was epic, and so was our sex. At the same time, we could be like little kids together, devoted soul mates. I moved in with him, and my life went from bohemian utopia to classic fairy tale. I'd never really wanted to have children before, but for the first time in my life, I was rethinking that decision. At the start of 2020 we'd picked out a ring and were trying to figure out the best time to plan our wedding. Then, everything went to hell. Like, everything.

Can we please time-lapse now through the horror show that was 2020? My version of that collective nightmare is that a dear friend of mine died from a long-term illness. Then my boss of sixteen years died suddenly from cancer. Then Bye Baby and I split up, and I moved out of his house and moved everything I owned into a storage unit. By 2021 my life as I'd known it was over. I spent the next few years dividing my time between LA and my hometown in the Pacific Northwest, trying to imagine, let alone build, some kind of new life for myself.

It would take a whole other book to describe that relationship and our subsequent breakup, but I'll say this much. Our huge love for each other was only one part of our story. I was both blind and not blind to the fact something was very wrong. I get it now—there was always an end waiting for us, and thank God it came sooner rather than later. That didn't make it any less excruciating.

I saw a billboard the other day that read, "Love always perseveres." I thought to myself, *That's not true. Sometimes love lets go.*

January 2019

I don't know what to make of this sex. It's no longer just for the sake of satisfying a hunger or to experience pleasure. It's a portal into union, an existence in which I am no longer separate and self-identified. It's a journey into together. We collide with one another, performing a kind of interior aerial ballet, encountering each other at our most raw and primal, meeting one another at the base of our Love.

March 2019

It's a rainy morning. We've had a lot of rainy mornings, and the backyard has turned into a jungle of green plants. We are so happy. But it's so much more than that. We connect at a level I didn't know was possible. I feel myself opening up to him—opening my heart—but it's like I'm finding my heart in all these nooks and crannies in my body. My heart exists in the sweetest deepest parts of me, and sometimes when we're having sex one of those places opens up to him and lets him in.

So, here I sit, typing this out for you, picturing the river that continues to raise me and how supernaturally green it can be. I'm fifty-two but feel and act like I'm seven. I continue to get older, yet inside I remain the same. How's that going to work going forward? I'm stepping again into a future not of my choosing but that chooses me. Writing this for you is the only thing I care about. Okay, that's not true. I love my family, I adore my friends. I love my morning coffee. I love flooding my body with pleasure. I really love learning new things. I love continuing to learn more about sacred sex.

Oh yeah, the part of my story I failed to mention. The minute I saw the writing on the wall with Bye Baby, I dove back into all the solo sexual cultivation practices I'd been learning before I met him. It was bizarre, but I knew this was what would save me. Why had I given it up in the first place? Oh, the irony. Being with a partner with whom I had interstellar sex had stalled me out on my personal evolution. That piece about me exploring and opening up new pathways in my body—in solitude—that had to go. I never felt comfortable saying, "Hey, I'm going to go, ah, self-pleasure for an hour, okay?" Now I picked up the trail of my erotic project where I'd left off three years before, for the first time 100% on my own.

Another thing I did as my world fell apart—I enrolled in a course at morrismethodsandmore.com on the embodied personal development methods of the late Dr. Glenn J. Morris, taught by Tao Semko. I was looking for relief from some bizarre physical issues I'd had for years. But the course opened up a whole new paradigm about the body and about physical energy. The timing could not have been more perfect. At the exact moment sex with a partner became not-an-option and also of no interest to me, I was launched into an exploration of the myriad realms of sensation possible within my own body. The course was not sexual at all, but it gave me a framework through which to understand all I'd been experiencing throughout my erotic project. I started to see that everything I'd experienced and learned is *known*. It may be mind-blowing to me, but it's known. As I keep saying, traditions around the world have studied the connection between sexual energy and vitality for millennia. Once that dawned on me, I couldn't believe regular people didn't know about this. I mean, we could all use some serious help here, living on this planet right now. We could all use a road map into this super power that lies inside us.

It's ironic that while writing this book, I've been essentially celibate. It doesn't bother me. Hopefully there will be plenty of sex in my future. There's still so much more to experience! For that I'll need a consistent partner (partners?). But the idea of sex sometimes bores me now. Amazing, I know. But what I want to know is this: What lies beyond conventional sex? What's beyond that supposedly supreme bliss of orgasm? That's where I'm headed, once this book is done.

For now, what intrigues me is what I've been going on about all this time. How do we imbue the moments of our lives with this wondrous elixir of our life force energy? How do we really *be* in these human bodies? Sex is great, but it's fleeting. How do we ignite within ourselves every day that which illuminates the magnitude of what it is to be here, now?

So, there you go. That's who I am, that's where I'm at.

How about you? How are you doing? Are you breathing? Do you still want to keep going here? Alright, enough already. Let's get back to it.

Whoops, I've got more to say. Some things you may or may not have identified about me. I'm strangely, boringly straight. I say strangely, because I'm a super sexual person! Why not have sex with everyone? It's not that I'm not open to the possibilities, but I always fall for men. I was hanging out with this guy in his seventies recently, a total Don Juan. We were like two mirrors facing each other. We'd been talking a long time—a meeting of the minds—swapping stories of love and passion, when he paused and made a toast: "I love women," he beamed. We clinked glasses, and I grinned back at him. "And I love men."

So, there you go.

I'm a cisgender woman. I identify with and present as the gender I was assigned at birth. That said, I do find the whole construct of gender utterly fascinating.

I'm white, another made-up thing that equals being super crazy privileged for no good reason. I'd love to ignore this, and the fact I could pretty much ignore it if I wanted to proves how privileged I am. In other ways, being white in a white supremacist society means I'm not quite fully developed, emotionally speaking. That's a heavy thing to say, but I mean it. I have blind-spots and assumptions. I know that much, but I don't even know what they all are, and I'll probably never know what the richness of life could be without them.

I'm middle class. I grew up not having to worry about money for the most part. My parents paid for me to go to college. I throw words around like free time and travel and investments like these are things we all have easy access to. I have had a labyrinthine journey with money, but I do have it pretty good.

Oh yeah, and I'm an American.

So, there you go. I'm one of the most advantaged people on the planet.

Given all that, I want you to know this book is for you, even if you and I are different from each other. If I offend you or I leave something out that's important to you, I'm really sorry. If this was a regular friendship you'd call me out on it and we'd talk and I'd apologize (oh, let's be real, people hardly ever get that honest with each other). Anyway, this is me apologizing up front for the ways in which I'm screwing up here.

Okay, shall we keep going? Are you still with me? Great! Maybe we'll make it all the way through this book together.

7
you can touch yourself

How are you feeling? Are you remembering to breathe?

In! And out.

All the way down into your pelvis.

Have you checked in with your wilderness recently? How's it feeling? In fact, how's your whole body feeling? If you had to pick one word, what would you say is the feeling tone in your body right now? Have you been outside yet today? Or moved your body at all? These are questions I hope you'll start asking yourself on a regular basis.

Okay, here's what's next on the menu:

I need you to touch yourself more.

That's right! You heard me.

Imagine if you had a partner and you never ever touched them. You never hugged them, never laid your hand on their arm or ran your fingers through their hair. That would be a sad relationship, right? Well, if you never ever touch yourself, that's the relationship you have with your own body.

This is pretty simple. Pick a part of your body and make physical contact. I'm not asking you to get naked (not if you don't feel like it), but how about stopping right now and giving yourself a great big bear hug? Come on! Set this book down for half a second and give yourself a great big squeeze.

Good.

Okay, now how about softly stroking the palm of your hand?

That feels nice, right?

Now, stroke and breathe at the same time.

Are you starting to notice that breathing makes everything better?

Oh, one more thing.

Smile.

This is very important! Just smile.

Lift up the corners of your mouth and smile into whatever part of your body has your attention right now—say, the palms of your hands. Look down at your palms right now. Imagine if you found the palms of your hands to be absolutely adorable. Smile at them. Smile *into* them. Smile into your palms like they're your beloved little pets. Beam love into them, smiling.

I'm not going make a fuss about it, but this last bit is one of those ancient secrets I'm dropping on you now like it's no big thing. We'll come back to this, but let's play around a little more with the palms of our hands.

practice: make love to your hand

Set a timer for 15 minutes.

Put your hands in your lap and let them rest there through this whole exercise.

Press the thumb of one hand into the palm of your other hand.

Go ahead and massage your whole palm. Get in there and squeeze around so it feels good.

Close your eyes and breathe.

I want you to explore your hand with your fingers like you're mapping it out. You're exploring the terrain of your own body, and you're doing it through the sense of touch.

Super super *super* slow.

Touch your hand in such a way you'd be embarrassed to have somebody watch you, because they'd think you were a weirdo. Go that slow. Be that attentive.

Run the finger of one hand slowly up the side of a finger of the other hand.

Slooowly.

Slower!

Even slower.

Feel what you're feeling.

Is one finger feeling this interaction more than the other?

Trace up and down, all around. Follow what feels good.

Go around to the back of the finger, stroke the nailbed, the cuticle.

Now, slide one fingernail slowly back and forth under the tip of another fingernail. There could be a bit of sensation there.

Breathe.

Slide fingers in between fingers.

Maybe you've discovered already it feels good to drag a fingernail across the skin.

Okay, now follow what feels good.

Slow down!

Allow yourself to drop down into a deep quiet place.

Allow the breath to settle.

Let yourself be surprised if this feels really really good.

I'm going to suggest there are layers of feeling within you, within your hand, that you've never accessed before. Am I right?

Play around and see.

This practice is inspired by an exercise from Betty Martin called *The Pleasure In Your Hands*.

I don't have a whole lot more to say about this touching-yourself thing. It's more of a doing thing. Sometimes waking up your body is as simple as giving yourself a good massage.

Here are a few more ways to connect with your body throughout the day.

- Palm your eyeballs (place the palms of your hands over your closed eyes) for fifteen seconds.
- Grab a finger and tug on it. That might feel so good you want to do it with each of your fingers. Or your toes.
- Pat yourself up and down on your thighs. Pat and breathe.
- Cup your neck with your hands and rest for a minute.
- Give yourself a shoulder rub.
- Lightly drum your fingers all over your scalp.
- Next time you take a shower, give yourself a leisurely scalp massage while you wash your hair.
- Slowly massage your belly.

- Oh, you want to know if you can touch yourself there? Of course you can! Geez, I hope you're touching yourself there. Smiling the whole time.

practice: give your breasts some love

It blows me away that every person on the planet does not know the profoundly healing practice of self breast massage. And yes, if you're a man, breast massage is something you can try out too. (Haha, I almost wrote *beast massage*).

There are a few ways you can do this. The shower or bathtub is often the best place to do it, because you're already naked and soaping up your boobs anyway. Why not give them a little love while you're at it? That said, you can do this anywhere. Let's try it now reclining in a chair or in bed propped up with some pillows.

Get some good organic oil, like sesame, jojoba, grapeseed, or coconut oil. You might want to have a towel or two on hand, since oil can stain things.

I pour some oil for starters on my sternum right in between my breasts (I recline rather than sitting up or lying all the way down, because it gives me more control over where all that oil goes).

Start by slathering the oil all around both your breasts. Really get it all over. You don't want to have to keep going back and getting more oil, because that's annoying.

Now, take the palm of one hand and trace a circle around one breast, going down on the outside of the breast and up on the inside. You could do this two-handed, with a breast in each hand, but that doesn't work for me, because I've got a big chest. What I do is trace around my breasts in the shape of a figure 8, so I'm always going down on the outside of the breast and up on the inside. It's like an infinity loop with each breast at the center of one of the loops.

Smile into your breasts as you do this (remember?). Blow them little air kisses. Tell them how much you love them.

Pinch your nipples, if you want.

Hi there!

Mwah mwah mwah.

This practice also comes from Taoist Inner Alchemy (also known as Nei Dan, internal alchemy, and alchemical Qigong) and was introduced to English-speaking readers by Mantak Chia along with the practice of The Inner Smile. This practice annoyed me when I first learned it because it made me aware of how little I could feel. I had almost no sensation at all in my breasts, and I'd joke that when a guy licked my nipples, I was like, *um, you do realize I feel nothing right now*. Over time though, I felt more and more sensation, and today breast massage is deeply nourishing and pleasurable for me.

In fact, it's one of the most powerful practices I've learned on my journey. Through it I discovered a warm and shiny state of self-love I didn't know was possible. At first it can feel strange to be this intimate with yourself, but once you get used to it, you can't get enough.

January 2018

I had absolutely no idea where this rabbit hole was gonna lead when I crept down inside it. I'm sure I still don't. I've sunk down so deep into myself. But this tenderness with myself—my pussy, my belly, my clit, my breasts, every inch of me from the inside out—I could never have known how precious this intimacy with myself would be.

It's reorienting my assumptions about pleasure, love, power, desire. Because all that is right here inside me. All of it. I don't get it from anywhere or anyone else. Couldn't get it from anyone else because it's right here. Within.

I felt so tender this morning, walking back to my car from his place. Like a baby goddess being birthed into being. And I'm like—What the hell am I doing here? What is this all about? All this pleasure? So, so, so much pleasure.

I looked up, and there was this giant image of a woman painted on the side of a building, gazing at me. She's been here this whole time. She's been looking out for me, beaming down on me. She's with me now, a physical representation of my endless unfolding.

8
be kind to yourself

Am I sensing some discomfort on your part? "Hey Heather, this is a lot of nakedness all of a sudden. I've gone from dancing around my living room like an idiot to slathering oil all over my breasts."

I hear you.

We've been conditioned to believe there's something bad about our bodies. Very bad. So *touching* our own bodies? And feeling pleasure while we touch ourselves? Yes, that can feel awkward at best.

Add to that all the memories our bodies hold. Touching ourselves can sometimes trigger an avalanche of feelings we weren't expecting. The memories connected to those feelings can be painful and even traumatic. If that's the case for you, and you happen to be one of the millions of people who've experienced sexual trauma, whatever you're feeling is of course completely okay and understandable. When we start to reconnect with our body, we often discover why we shut that connection to ourselves down in the first place. Opening up again can be a long, slow process.

We're not trying to fake feeling good here. We're learning to be with what is. So, if what is is some major freakout, do your best to love yourself through what you're feeling. I don't want to be a big downer here, but sometimes the path to pleasure involves unearthing and healing some serious abuse and trauma first. I'm not an expert in this. I've simply witnessed that this can come up for people as they get back in touch with their sexual selves. I don't want you to be shocked if that's the case for you. Is there a friend you can call? Can you reach out to a therapist for support? Do whatever you can to take exquisite care of yourself.

If touching yourself brings up too much right now, go back to the breath. It's always here for you. Go back to the other practices of moving your body and of savoring your food, which we'll explore soon. Ground yourself by getting outside and going for a walk. You can come back to these more sensual practices any time if you decide you want to. Or not.

And on that note, let's talk about consent. Yes, consent.

"But Heather, it's just me here. What does consent have to do with anything?"

Let me tell you a story. I was learning what's called a yoni egg practice where you insert a smooth stone or crystal in the shape of an egg into your pussy and do exercises to increase sensation and dexterity. At the beginning of each exercise you were supposed to let the egg rest against your vulva and ask your body for permission to insert the egg. Now, typically by this point I'd already gone to a lot of trouble to find some free time and get undressed and get my oil and prep my egg. A voice in my head would be like, "Yeah, no. We're not asking for permission here. We're doing this." I'd stick the egg inside me and get started.

It took a long time for me to realize how mean I was being to my own body. When I finally heard myself, I was shocked.

How many times have you agreed to have sex because it's easier than saying you don't feel like it, or because you want the other person to be satisfied, or you're not ready but you don't want to "take too long" to get turned on? Yeah, me too. So many times. Then there are all those times I've ignored my gut and gone to an event or even just answered the phone because I thought I should. No wonder I'm conditioned to override my feelings. I do it to myself 24/7.

Stopping and truly listening to your body is a powerful act. Asking yourself what you want, then taking the time to listen for a response. Sometimes the response isn't clear. Now, that's annoying. Can you sit with that too? Can you be patient and kind with yourself when you're not sure what it is you feel or what you want?

It was a huge deal for me to finally listen to my own body. Today, if I don't feel like sticking a stone egg inside my vagina, I don't do it. I'd call that progress, wouldn't you?

It's not only okay, it's fantastic if you realize you don't want to do something or if something feels like too much. Be thankful that your body is communicating with you. Honor what it wants and needs. See what it feels like to be that nice to yourself.

The yoni egg has got a lot of bad press in recent years. To be sure, it's not some magical cure-all, but it is a phenomenal practice. If you feel called to try it, I recommend taking a course with the founder of the modern jade egg movement, Dr. Saida Désilets.

Choosing to work with a teacher is another place where you need to honor both your intuition and your critical thinking skills. I've seen some "gurus" over the course of my journey, and all I have to say about that is Beware! There are a lot of people out there looking to boost their egos and build their empires off your yearning for expansion. In the realm of sexual energy in particular, that can get ugly. You really do need to watch out for people (of any gender) who claim to be sages, then suggest you need to have sex with them or someone they know, or you need to hand over your life savings in order to attain enlightenment. That's not enlightenment. That's sexual/spiritual abuse. I'd love it if we didn't need to discuss this issue, but it's important you understand the need for caution if you choose to venture as I did into the wilds of the sacred sex industry. Research whomever you choose to study with and be discerning as you work with them. Always locate your power within yourself. Never hand it over to another person, no matter how spiritually evolved you think they are. This is really important.

Remember when I was talking to my pussy? In case you didn't notice, I described your wilderness as a place of wisdom. I could have described your whole body as a place of wisdom, but when you're first learning to talk to your body, it helps to have one clear point of contact. Talking to your wilderness is a great place to start.

practice: ask your wilderness

Think of a decision you need to make, something that can be answered with a yes or a no. For now, let it be something low-stakes like, *Do I want to call so-and-so back now?*

Close your eyes.

Take a deep breath.

In—and out.

Place a hand on your belly or on your wilderness.

Now, pose the question directly to your wilderness.

Hey, wilderness, do you want to call so-and-so right now?

Or

Would you like to go grocery shopping now?

Or

Do you want to go outside?

You might listen for an UH-HUH or an UH-UH coming from deep within you.

Or you might feel for a shift—a feeling of light, upward motion throughout your body (indicating a yes) or a stuck, compressed feeling (a no).

You may feel totally blank, or maybe there's too much noise in your head to get a clear response. That's okay. Try this practice off and on. *Hey wilderness, would you like to go to that lecture at the library on the historical consequences and geopolitical implications of deep-sea diving in the late-twentieth century?* Or *Hey wilderness, would you like to just go ahead and eat this bowl of what might possibly be spoiled fruit?*

The important thing for starters is to ask your body a question and listen for its answer. You may not always like the answer, and you may not always honor it. Just notice when you go against what your body wants. How does that feel? Over time, you will learn more and more to not only listen to your wilderness but to also act (or not act) in accordance with what it tells you.

April 2017
I start crying. Really, really, dam-breaking crying. You ask me, "Do you want to stop?" I say no and put my hands on your back. The powerful sadness at all the times I was dragged to the finish line. All the times this was no fun at

all. All the times my climax was a medal to be hung around someone else's neck until I couldn't do it at all. And even now, the slightest hint you want to make me come, and my whole body goes dark. So, I'm crying, and we keep going, which is weird, but it feels right and it's a quiet finish and you tell me that at the end you finally landed in your body.

9
consecration

Are you starting to grasp what we're doing? We're tracking your life force energy like it's an elephant in the wild. It's in there somewhere. It's just a matter of finding it and waking it up.

Remember, your journey began by taking a deep breath in and out, all the way down into your wilderness. Then you checked in with your wilderness to see how it was doing. In the process, you discovered how to return to that whole-body sense of being in your own skin, that state of innocent aliveness. Next, you circulated sensation and feeling and awareness all through yourself in a big orbit. You got your blood pumping by dancing or going for a walk or getting outside. And you touched yourself! You gave yourself a big hug or maybe you even took the time to massage your breasts. Now you're learning to listen to your body and practice consent with yourself.

So, now what?

Now we're going to go back to our simmering pot of water on the stove. And we're going to gently, gently turn up the heat underneath that pot.

What we're going for is a sense of aliveness in the body. As you can see, you can stoke that fire by waking up your nipples or by breathing into your wilderness. There's an enormous amount of energy in these erogenous zones! But let me remind you, none of this has to be blatantly sexual. In fact, if you think it has to be anything at all, take a step back and relax. The invitation here is not to take on yet another agenda to make yourself a better person or a better lover. This isn't about that at all. The invitation is to return to your body, to be here with yourself, wherever you are right now.

Alright, if you're down for even more nakedness, here's a beautiful practice that is super soothing and nourishing.

practice: anoint yourself

You'll need at least fifteen minutes and a private place to lie down.

Get your oil. (Organic sesame is good for this one, but hey, use what you've got).

Lay a towel down on your bed, the sofa, or the floor.

Make sure the room is warm enough for you to feel comfortable.

Get naked and lie down.

Take the oil and slather it on your belly. Take your time and gently smooth it over your skin in circles. Play with smaller circles, then larger ones.

Enjoy the feeling of the oil on your skin.

Now smooth that liquid down into the creases of your hips. You can use the edges of your hands to dig in a little bit—get into those hip flexors.

Massage your groin (your groin includes your pelvis as well as the area between your pelvis and your inner thighs), smooth down the inner lines of your legs, all the way down to your ankles.

You can do this lying down on your back with your legs bent up in the air so you can reach your ankles more easily. Or sit up and reach down.

Get more oil if you need it.

Make slow meditative circles around your inner ankle bones, focusing pressure especially on the hollows under the knobs of the ankles.

Work your way back up your inner calves, your inner thighs, back to your groin.

Take a minute to softly smooth your fingers over your wilderness, lovingly massaging that whole area.

If you have time, you can continue upwards, massaging up from the belly, up to the breasts, circling the breasts with the palms of your hands. Stay here for a while.

Now, continue massaging gently up the sides of your neck, up to your face. Massage your cheeks, underneath the cheekbones, where the muscles of the jaw come together. Now slide your fingers back from there toward your ears and massage the little flap of cartilage directly in front of your ear canal (it's called the tragus). Gently press or tug on it.

Let this whole massage be slow and steady and rhythmic.

You should feel softer, smoother, more in tune with yourself.

This is a massage of the Yinqiao Extraordinary Meridians created by Tao Semko. The Yinqiao (a Classical Chinese Medicine term) helps with grounding, embodiment, accessing embodied emotions and sensations, and connection between people. This is a great massage for soothing yourself if you feel an anxious nervy energy around the prospect of sexual connection. It's also great if you've got a lot of pelvic sexual energy and you're feeling a lot of pent-up desire in one area. Doing this helps to spread it over that entire area. It's also just good when you feel like your brain wants to fly off into the stratosphere.

The oil is key here. It's very grounding for the body.

You can anoint yourself in simple ways too.

Drop a dab of oil on the palm of each hand and massage your hands.

Or take a minute before bed and rub some oil into your feet.

Or you can do the real deal anointment thing and use your middle finger to touch a drop of oil to the space between your eyebrows.

May 2021

Funny thing. Here I am, writing a blog on sex and sexuality, feeling this calling to share with others how to have more satisfying and pleasurable sex. But I myself am a little tapped out on the whole sex thing.

I mean, my relationship did just end. So that could have something to do with it. You think?

But you know what? Even before it ended, and after three years of truly epic sex, I was starting to wonder what I guess a lot of people ask at some point:

Is there more?

It feels sacrilegious to say this, but, I mean, how many times can your body detonate with a pleasure that sears you from the soles of your feet to the top of your head? How many times? Ten times? Fifty? Hundreds of times? My god, even sexual ecstasy—like every other thing in life—even this can become routine?

Today, pleasure for me is something quiet and interior. It doesn't look like much. I don't know what to make of it. I keep doing all these breathing exercises, and all I know is when I do them I feel soothed and whole. I'm able to bear my grief. I feel quiet, powerful, connected, and I'm in the flow. Right now there's just not knowing and surrender.

10
receiving pleasure

LIFE IS A BANQUET, LAID OUT FOR YOU EVERY DAY.
PLEASURE IS EVERYWHERE.
YOUR MORNING SHOWER, THE WARM WATER TUMBLING OVER YOUR SKIN.
HOT COFFEE.
A WALK.
BREATHING DEEP.
SMILING INTO YOUR BODY.
RUNNING SENSATION THROUGH YOU IN LITTLE RIVULETS OF WARM HONEY.
IN THE CAR, IN A MEETING, AT THE STORE.
ALWAYS, IN EACH AND EVERY MOMENT, YOU ARE BUZZING WITH LIFE.
CAN YOU FEEL IT?

Let's talk about receiving pleasure. I throw that word around a lot, and you might think what I mean by that is just sexual pleasure. Of course, sex is one way to feel very good, but you know yourself there are so many more. There's the pleasure of feeling the sun on your skin or of tasting a juicy plum in the middle of summer. How about the thrill of a terrific conversation, the sweetness of spending time with those you love?

Are you able to be present for what's here in this moment? Maybe it's not pleasure. Maybe it's something else. Grief. Or blankness. Discomfort. Pain. Rage. That's okay, be present for all that too. But when the opportunity arises to feel good—when you're eating a special meal or you're taking a bath—can you enjoy it? Are you even here to enjoy it?

When I was about a year into my erotic project I became obsessed with this question: *How do you receive pleasure?* Meaning: *Why can't I enjoy my life?* The life I was living was extraordinary. I had a few lovers and was inundated with kisses, with foot massages and pussy massages (oh, yes), with long meandering conversations and sex and lots of snuggling. I had wonderful friends I dearly loved. I was writing furiously whenever I could find a minute. My life was suffused with goodness, but somehow I couldn't fully receive it. It was like I was the gatekeeper to my own pleasure, but I wouldn't let myself in.

What irked me most was my home. I couldn't fully relax in it anymore. The minute Ex #1 (Honey Pie) moved out, I became uncomfortable living in such a beautiful place all by myself. Now, we're not talking a mansion here. This was basically a very nice cabin I was renting in the canyons north of LA, but it was a special place, tucked into a ravine, looking out at a sweeping hillside where the birds sang their hearts out in the mornings. Once it was just me living there, it felt like too much beauty for one person. The brilliant green vines trailing outside the windows, the sun shimmering on the trees, the burble of the big stone fountain outside. I felt awkward living there by myself, unable to settle back in or claim the place as my own.

I was also overwhelmed trying to manage my newly exploding love life. After years of famine, it was feast time. But more partners meant more people's schedules and emotions to negotiate, and I found myself skittering over the surface of my life, struggling to make it all work. It's hilarious now to think how much time I spent bemoaning how overwhelmed I was. I didn't have the bandwidth to take it all in.

Once I identified what was going on with me, I of course immediately tried to wrestle the issue to the ground. I dove into yet more courses, more books. I grilled people I considered experts on the subject of receiving. I once walked up to a woman I knew at a Tantra workshop and said, "You *know* something I don't about receiving pleasure! It's written all over your face. How do you do it?" I'm not making this up. I really said this to her. She smiled back at me like she was the Mona Lisa and said nothing. Yes, I was a crazy person, but through that quest, I soaked up a lot of the wisdom that's now become second nature to me.

What I learned over time was simple. The capacity to receive pleasure is developed through your *presence* and your *appreciation*. Just, you know, appreciating shit. Oh right, and also that thing we just talked about—knowing (or considering that *maybe*) you are worthy of feeling good.

In case you missed it, that last paragraph was huge. You should flag that or write it down or make it your home screen or something.

I am worthy of feeling good.

If this statement rings false to you, play around with it a little bit. Let it become a koan of sorts, banging around in your head.

Am I worthy of feeling good?

Maybe I am worthy of feeling good.

It's possible I am worthy of feeling good.

Pleasure can be found in just about anything if you pay attention. Beauty rituals are one great way to do this. Smoothing lipstick across your lower lip, patting moisturizer into your skin, dabbing some sparkle on your cheeks. The body comes alive with this kind of attention.

But even something as mundane as washing dishes becomes a smorgasbord for the senses when you allow yourself to be present for it. First, there's all that warm soapy water sloshing around. All those little bubbles. There's the clinking of cups, the sleek wetness of a plate, the elegant lines of the silverware heavy in your hands. The sudsing, the rinsing. There can be something so meditative and sensually satisfying about the whole experience.

Pleasure must be sought, but don't go looking for it. Seek it out where it is—right here. Once you find it, do your very best to let it in.

This very moment—your eyes scanning this page or your ears hearing these words—can be a portal into pleasure. You pass through it or not, depending on the quality of your attention. Can you allow yourself to be curious, to be startled? What colors do you see in your peripheral vision right now? If you breathe in, do you smell anything? How does your tongue feel against the back of your teeth?

Now that you've dropped in and are present, is there something you appreciate about this moment? If so, the next step is to enjoy the hell out of it. Really relish your experience. You can do this all through the day. Mark the moment for yourself by giving voice to what you appreciate. Say out loud as you slip into your favorite flannel pj's, "Oh, these feel nice!" Tell your friend how you couldn't stop laughing while watching that show she told you about. Before bed, write down one thing you appreciated today. Acknowledging, describing, reveling in what pleases you makes it easier to experience even more and more pleasure.

Eating is another great way to practice this. You have to eat every day anyway. And savoring a meal is an ancient and deeply human way to dig in to the succulence of being alive.

practice: the blueberry & the alien

Go in the kitchen and grab one bite of something to eat. Say, one blueberry.

(It can be anything really: a section of orange, a square of chocolate, a pickle slice, whatever).

Put it on a plate, and sit down in a quiet place with the plate in front of you.

Close your eyes and take a minute to be still and breathe.

Now, open your eyes.

Imagine you're an alien from another planet and you've never encountered a blueberry before. You have no idea what this tiny sphere is in front of you.

Pick up the little blue orb.

Hold it in your hand and really look at it. What do you see?

Roll it gently between your fingers.

Pass it from one palm to the other.

Sniff it.

Go ahead and put it in your mouth, but don't bite into it yet. Let it rest there on your tongue.

Feel its smooth tautness.

Take your time!

Finally, take a bite and notice that little pop as you puncture its plump skin.

The lush tart sweetness, that little explosion in your mouth.

Now, swallow.

Does this feel like an exercise in mindfulness? That's because it is! Long before My Big Sexual Revolution, I lived and practiced for seven years at the Zen Center of Los Angeles, a Zen Buddhist Temple in the heart of LA. Before that, I learned to meditate at the Zen Community of Oregon, and that's where I learned this practice from Jan Chozen Bays. As it turns out, this kind of sensory contemplation is also a basic Tantric exercise.

When you feel physically shut down, appreciating your food can be a great inroad back into your body. Think about it: Food is so tactile, so fragrant. Even if you feel numb inside, you can still taste. You can still smell.

Even that cup of coffee in your hand.

Does it feel heavy? Light?

What does the lip of the cup feel like as you press it to your mouth? Is it hot? Or just warm?

Where does the flavor land on your tongue as you take a sip? On the front? On the sides of your tongue? The back?

Isn't that interesting?

You can bring this kind of attention to your very first bite of food every time you sit down (or stand in front of the fridge) to eat. All you have to do is remember to pause. Take a split second as you sink your teeth into that first bite, roll it around in your mouth and taste it. Follow the flavors as they cascade through your mouth in a sequence. What does the food feel like in your mouth? Does the texture change as you chew it? What happens when you swallow? Can you track the food as it travels from your mouth, down your throat, into your stomach?

Really commit to always tasting that first bite of food. You could try eating mindfully through a whole meal, but since I can't manage that myself, I'm not going to tell you to do it. But try slowing down the next time you eat, doubling how long it would normally take you to finish your meal. Make a game out of it and chew each bite of food eleven times before you swallow. This will feel awkward at first. I mean, what are you going to do? Just sit there? Well, you're going to taste your food. And if you're with friends or family you might, um, talk to them.

Cooking, too, can be its own sumptuous experience. When you allow yourself to drop into the pleasure of cooking, it's like entering another world. There's a sixth sense that kicks in. You just know when the pasta is done, you can sense how much salt the soup needs, you're inspired to add a squeeze of lime at the last minute. This quality of presence can carry over into the rest of your life, creating its own kind of afterglow.

You might think based on what I've written here that I'm some master of mindful eating. That's not the case. I have a very, ah, complex relationship with food. As with sex, I got a lot of mixed messages about eating growing up. We prefer now to call it *clean eating* instead of *dieting*, but we're still presented with this ever-changing list of "bad" and "good" foods. And we're still supposed to be at war with the bad ones. The thing is, you can never win that war. Defeat's always one slip away in the kitchen or at the checkout line.

But oh, to truly love food? To sink your teeth into an orange and savor its succulence? Or a slice of chocolate cake? Oh, no. Etiquette requires numerous jokes about how bad you're being, how sinful this is, how much you're going to regret this.

If I wanted, I could give a sermon on how those of us living in the U.S. have been impacted by the assumptions embedded in American culture by the Puritans who settled here a few centuries ago. Our attitudes toward food and sex and really anything at all that's pleasurable can't be untangled from their peculiar convictions.

Whenever I talk about the primacy of pleasure, I imagine my own ancestors from down the centuries and across wildly different branches of my family tree—some of them literally Puritans, others connected to the earth and to their bodies—debating this subject with each other. Some of them must be horrified now by what I'm writing. Others, I know, are cheering me on.

Here's the sermon I'd offer them, if I could. It's basically the message of this whole book. The sermon would be this: *Your Desire Is Holy*.

What were we talking about again? Oh right, food! While I've dodged the worst of our collective war on eating, it still creeps into my life in insidious ways. When I eat something I love, I don't actually taste it. I shovel it from plate to mouth and gulp it down from mouth to belly, and somewhere in there the experience of savoring the flavors of the food is lost.

One day I realized—I never really get to eat chocolate. Oh sure, I put it in my mouth, but I don't let myself *taste* it! I swallow it before I have the chance to even register I'm eating it. Here I am, depriving myself of one of my very favorite things, even though technically I am eating the chocolate.

What is the solution here? What's the remedy for this insanity?

Well, slowing down, to start.

Maybe even stopping.

Allowing myself to be here.

To feel, taste, enjoy this.

This bite of chocolate, this air in my lungs, this bath, this skin on skin, this fuzzy robe, this belly laugh.

Receiving. All of it.

One last thing! Totally random, I know, but I have to give a quick shout out to the sense of smell! The ineffable evocative potency of smell.

Can we take a minute here to be in awe at the power of scent to elevate a moment or unlock a memory? Different smells evoke such different experiences within us. Conjure now in your imagination the smell of leather

vs. from the smell of smoke

vs. from the smell of roses

or pepper.

Then there's the whole world of perfumes and candles and essential oils and incense you can play around with—all the scented things that imbue a space with a halo of warmth. There are the smells of the natural world—damp earth, the smell before a thunderstorm, the smell of the ocean. I could go on and on. An entire ode to smell! Sagebrush, pine trees, the smell of sweat.

Then there's your very own scent. Do you even know what you smell like? Have you ever reached down and touched yourself, then smelled your finger?

Too much? Okay, file that one away for later. But aren't you curious now? I mean, I don't know about you, but I love the smell of my lover. Why wouldn't I love the smell of myself too?

I'm inching into dangerous territory here, I know. Territory that bucks a hundred years or so of the mass marketing of hygienic and feminine products. Whatever. You know what, I'll take it one step further. Don't just smell your finger.

Taste it!

June 2019

Our sex this morning was decadent. And then. You made me coffee with whipped cream! You made it from raw whole cream and added vanilla to it and whipped and whipped and whipped at it as I lounged in the bathtub wondering what it was you were doing. You brought it to me in the tub, and when I felt the foam on my lips and tasted the vanilla on my tongue I was so happy.

But the sex.

We're diving into it again and again, surfing that sensation. Diving down into the lusciousness, the saltiness. Today I hit a roll of laughter like low thunder right before I came. I come now like a raging torrent. And this is when I enter an altered state, half here half there, only who knows where there is. Gone over into daylight or moonlight, eyes rolled back to meet the sunshine behind my own eyelids. I open my eyes and seek you again, seek to be present with you, to be in this together as we are.

See, here's the thing. I'm writing about sex. But I can't write this. I can't share this. And yet this is what is. This is what I mean when I say I've had a sexual awakening. This is what I mean when I tell you a miracle has occurred. This is what I mean when I say I'm so very happy.

11
the voice

There's that voice in the back of my head right now.

How dare you talk of pleasure? Look at this world. Look at it. Look at the horror, the injustice, the devastation.

Do you know, for a long time I couldn't enjoy taking a shower. I was plagued with guilt for the extravagance of an endless stream of hot water when there are people here in the U.S. and all over the world who don't have water they can safely bathe in or even drink.

I mentioned this to a friend of mine, this kind of curse hovering over me when I ate a good meal knowing others were hungry. Or how I couldn't stop thinking of all those people without hot water.

My friend is known for speaking her mind, and she blurted out, "How dare you?! You have hot water. They don't. *Someone* in this world should be enjoying that hot water! Do you think for one second they wouldn't revel in such a luxury if they could? How dare you not appreciate what millions of people would give so much to experience? How ironic, how tragic is it that you—who actually have the hot water—can't enjoy it?"

I still don't know for sure if she was right about that. But I do take my shower now thankfully, with joy. I allow the heat to soak deep into my pores. I don't know how to explain it, but her outrage cured me.

There's so much suffering in this world, beyond comprehension. Some of us do what we can to call for peace and justice. Some even work hard for it. But in the midst of it, we all live our lives. Don't we? We do. We live our lives.

I called that friend up again just now. I told her what I'm writing. "How can I talk about pleasure, given this world we're living in? How do I dare to do it?"

She said to me, "Heather, you do it *because* of this world we're living in."

practice: smile from the back of your brain

Remember your inner smile?

Let's play around with that a little more. We're going to try something different. This time, rather than smiling into a part of your body, why don't you try just smiling? A very faint, barely perceptible, turning up of the corners of your mouth. Think the Mona Lisa. Think the Buddha. A smile so subtle, only you know it's there.

Imagine the smile originating from the back of your skull. Yes. Go ahead and put your hand back there, just above the base of your neck. Cradle the back of your skull and feel it smiling. You could even picture a holographic happy face beaming away back there.

Walk around like this for a while. Your eyes softened and dropped down and back a bit toward that smile in the back of your skull.

How do you feel?

In the same way that you can always return to your breath, you can remember this smile in the back of your brain and allow it to coax the corners of your mouth up ever so slightly. This practice was created by Tao Semko as a way to elicit a genuine smile. It's the opposite of that thing we do to make nice by turning up the corners of the mouth. As you can see, it feels pretty good.

April 2022
In one hundred years, each of us will have lived out our time on this earth—forever—in these particular human bodies. From here we'll go on to something else. And the kicker is, we don't know what that something else is, so all we've got is this.

We're walking along the edges of the mystery, feeling our way. There are moments where we keep putting one foot in front of the other, not knowing where we are. There are moments of blazing brilliance where we're startled into the memory that something big is going on. All the time, we never really know. How could we? We dip a toe into the mystery. If we're lucky, sometimes we're allowed to enter.

12
circulating pleasure

We're at a jumping-off point now on our journey together. Before we move forward, I want to check in and see how you're doing. How are you feeling? Are you feeling a little more *in* your body? Are you able to find and bask in some things that make you feel good? This is important, because the rest of this book is about how to take a pleasurable sensation within you and expand that sensation throughout the whole force field that is your body.

So I want to make sure we're on the same page at this point. Have you tried out some of the practices? Be honest! No judgement here, but if not, I encourage you to go back and try one out now. Just pick one! It'll take you ten minutes. There's no comparison between reading something on a page and feeling it in your body. If you can't think of which thing to try, go back to that list in Chapter 7 of simple ways you can play around with your sense of touch.

If you have tried some practices and you're not feeling much yet, that's okay. Keep at it. It can take a while (quite a while in some cases) for the body to come back to life. Keep breathing, keep reaching for pleasure.

Now let's take that pleasure and start to circulate it throughout the body. As always, we begin with the breath. Is this starting to sink in for you? The breath is your way *in* to pleasure. It's the master key to the palace.

One more time, let's take one big deep breath in—all the way down!—and let it out.

Breathing wakes things up; it gets everything moving! Once you're feeling something—anything—you can ride those effervescent bubbles of heightened sensation all through your body, following the movement with your breath. This doesn't have to be a big thing. It can be very subtle, but subtle can feel divine.

You're riding a wave, basically, and you can ride that wave while you brush your teeth, watch TV, cook dinner, sit in traffic and yes, while you're having sex.

Again, all this is already happening inside of you. You're not making oxygen disperse through your blood or making that blood flow through your capillaries. You're not directing the flow of hormones through your body or telling your food to digest itself. These things happen every millisecond of your life without you doing a single thing. That's because you are *pulsing* with life! Tap into the mystery of that. Tap into the wonder of that. Allow the awareness of this miracle of being alive to quietly change you.

You can breathe absolutely any feeling through your body. For example, you could breathe in a feeling of oneness with nature. Let's try it.

practice: five gates breathing

Stand up.

Oh, come on already, get up!

Plant your feet hip-width apart and slightly bend your knees.

Feel yourself grounding down into the earth. Picture a giant tree root going down from your tailbone, straight down into the ground below you.

Imagine roots springing from that root, spreading down, down, down all the way to the very core of the earth.

Imagine a root springing out of each of your feet as well, rooting down.

Now, breathe in earth energy all the way up from the center of the earth.

Breathe it up through your roots, up through your feet, your legs, up into your belly.

As you get up to your chest, exhale that earth energy through your outspread arms, out through the palms of your hands and your fingertips, out to the sides of your body.

Breathe in again, this time inhaling the energy of all of life, the trees, the birds, animals and plants. Breathe this life force energy in through the palms of your hands, through your wrists and arms, back into the center of you.

Now, breathe out through the top of your head. *Gently.* Like you're a whale with a blowhole, and you're softly breathing this life force energy out the top of your head up to the stars and the cosmos.

Breathing in again, draw in that cosmic stardust energy gently down through the blowhole in the top of your head, down through your heart, through your belly and legs and . . . breathe it down through the soles of your feet, back down into the earth.

Breathe in earth energy again, in through your feet.

And repeat!

This is a Qigong practice. The "five gates" of this practice refer to your two feet + two hands + your head. You can switch the sequence up by breathing in through your arms and out through your feet, or in through your feet and out straight up through the top of your head, etc.

It feels amazing to do this in the woods or at the ocean. If you can, play with this in your backyard or at a park. The added feedback you'll get from the sun, rain, air, trees and dirt will help you feel the flow of the elements through you. If you feel self-conscious, don't make it a big thing. Do it as you walk through the park, swinging your arms as you go, breathing that energy in and through you. Experiment with just how much energy is available to you in any moment, simply by tuning in to the breath.

Now, don't go crazy with this one! When I say breathe gently, I mean *gently*! As you do this exercise you're going to feel how much energy is available to you, and you might feel tempted to get all superhero on me and huff and puff and breathe the hell out of this. Don't get greedy and try to stuff yourself with more energy than your system can handle. Slow and easy really is the way to go.

I learned a number of the practices in this book from my mentor and friend, Tao Semko. I started studying with Tao in 2021, through that online course I mentioned at Morris Methods and More.

The course became a lifeline for me as I navigated the grief of my breakup with Bye Baby (Ex #2). The breathing techniques soothed my nervous system and helped me process what at the time felt like unbearable loss.

Tao ("thay-oh") is a true teacher. He has immense respect and tenderness for his students, and vice versa. I'd tell you he's one of the most enlightened people I know, but even that modest description would make him visibly cringe. As a true teacher, he discourages any hint of adulation. But seriously, when Tao is happy, it's like his whole being beams. He's beyond generous with his wisdom and his encyclopedic wealth of knowledge. I've never seen a question phase him. He's also very fun to talk to.

By late 2021 I was doing a daily Morris Methods practice and routinely dropping into what I can only describe as an ecstatic state. At first it felt like I'd gone completely off course from my erotic project. Not only was I no longer having sex, the Morris Methods material wasn't sexual at all. Instead, it felt like an endless series of mundane exercises I was strangely inspired to do every single day. Over time, I began to experience these states of bliss on par with what I'd encountered at the beginning of my sexual revolution. It didn't make any sense. How could breathing be blissful? It took a while to realize I was still on the same path I'd started out on all those years ago. I hadn't veered off of it, but the map I'd been using didn't include the whole path! Not even a fraction of it. I'd been so focused on sexual ecstasy, I forgot ecstasy comes in countless other forms.

I read a ton of books, trying to gain some context for what I was experiencing. I read a lot about Tantra and Taoist Inner Alchemy in particular. I learned that Tantra is a far more vast and nuanced system than what's typically practiced today. What we think of now as Tantra is really what's called Neotantra, and that's mainly focused on sex. But Tantra in its entirety is about consciousness.

When you think of the word "consciousness," you might think about your mind or your spirit or your capacity to think. But Tantra understands consciousness to be much vaster than that. Here, it is the interplay between energy, matter, and the numinous (or spirit). This interplay occurs along a continuum through time and space. Consciousness is not just a cerebral or even a spiritual thing. It's rooted in our very lives, in this physical world we find ourselves in right now, and also beyond this world.

The word *tantra* comes from the same root in Sanskrit as the word for weave, loom, or web. It implies the interconnectedness of all things. The way I see it, it's about All That Is seeking to know itself better. Sometimes we say things like "I'm a part of all that is" or "The drop of water doesn't know it's part of the whole ocean." Well, I'm that drop of water seeking to know myself as ocean. And the ocean is seeking to know itself as me.

Both Tantra and Taoism (of which Taoist Inner Alchemy is one branch) are complex philosophical systems that have developed over thousands of years. Tantra is often described as emerging around the 6th century AD, but it's a philosophy and set of practices that developed in India long before that (as we can see in ancient art and artifacts).

As for Taoism, while it's popularly known as the Chinese philosophy of the oneness of all things, Taoist Inner Alchemy is one branch of Taoism that's a path or technology for internal transformation. One of the earliest texts describing its processes was written in 320 AD by Ko Hung. Those processes involve cultivating sexual energy, working with the elements of nature, and channeling the flow of energy through the body.

Am I overwhelming you? Don't worry! You don't have to venture onto some psychic sensual metaphysical odyssey like me. You don't need to read a million books. You can just try things out and have a nice pleasurable sensation of more flow in your body.

That said, it was pretty amazing what I experienced during those months of intense practice. One of these days I'll return to it. Since then, I've fallen away from my Morris Methods practice and returned to a more mundane existence (you know, living, working, writing a *book*). Still, I want to share with you some of what I experienced during that extraordinary time when I was so deeply dropped into my body.

May 2022

I find myself on this deep dive into: What exactly is Tantra? I'm familiar at this point with a lot of Tantric practices and some of the philosophy, but it's still a great mystery to me what Tantra is.

I'm banging on this door, pounding and yelling. Hey! Let me in! On some level I know I'm pounding on the door of my own wisdom. I keep reminding myself I'm on a quest. There's a whole frontier of feeling out there beyond climax that I'm reaching for.

This morning I listened to the rain and felt myself expand, becoming a part of it. My edges vanished, and I was the rainstorm. That was all the pleasure I could want this morning. I never felt anything like this before. Nothing sexual about it and yet experiencing myself physically as part of the whole of everything. Of the sky, the trees, the earth.

As I read more about Tantra, I find this is, in fact, what it's all about. This oneness with life. It's like Zen meditation, but in this full-body ecstatic sense.

I know I'm on the brink of an epic expansion. I'm not afraid even though this is all unfamiliar, even though the boundaries of me have expanded far beyond the edges of my body. I simply float into this sensation that's always been available. I just wasn't aware of it before.

Now, I feel the surface of my skin against the air after a long bath. There's no division between me and this air, me and the cosmos. I experience all this through my body instead of reaching for it in my mind. I am flow within the flow.

Okay, maybe I am a little scared. I sense there's no returning to my previous experience of the world once I cross this threshold. It reminds me of my former fear of impending orgasm. The hugeness of it, uncontrollable and unknown. Once and again and always the answer is surrender. Surrender to this.

After months of belly breathing, baby's breath breathing, five-point breathing, elemental breathing . . . After all this freaking breathing, now simply taking a breath in and out I feel the whole surface of my body come alive.

I wish I had a lover to reflect all this back to me, so we could look into each other's eyes and marvel My God. Instead it's just me and the trees, me and the moon, me and this Earth smiling in astonishment. But I'm the only one who's astonished; the Universe is well versed in this. I'm finally open to receiving all of it.

Let's go back now to that wave of sensation we were talking about—you can breathe that wave through you like it's literally a wave on the ocean. You could also breathe it through you as a fluffy-cotton-candy wave or like twinkling gold (remember your Macrocosmic Orbit?) You could breathe a cool, soothing breeze through you or a warm current of honey. You see where I'm going with this. There are infinite ways to circulate pleasure through your body. From here on out, all the practices except one are those I've created myself, through trial and error. Here's a fun one.

practice: the breath as your lover

Imagine your breath is a sensuous mist traveling through your body.

Breathe in, allowing the mist to envelop your body like some mystical lover.

Whisper the breath through you.

Let it caress you, stirring you from the inside out.

See where it goes.

Flare your nostrils and feel the air travel through your nasal passages and down through your throat.

Imagine it doesn't just fill your lungs but instead spreads down into your fingertips, into the palms of your hands.

Let it travel all the way down to your toes and enliven the soles of your feet.

Let it spiral delicately up through the top of your head or spiderweb out through the whole front surface of your body.

Let it brush across your lips and your eyelashes and your ear lobes.

Don't worry here about what elemental energies you're breathing in and out. Just focus on breathing in and out from all five "gates," letting the energy flow through you. Do this *softly*. No pushing! Let it be a gentle flow.

March 2023
I was complaining to Tao the other day how I still have no idea what I'm writing about. I'm writing about sex, I'm not writing about sex. I'm writing about sexual energy, but

what is that anyway and how does it differ from plain old energy?

He suggested my dilemma is living in this world that wants to compartmentalize sex and sexuality and put it in its own little box. Instead of acknowledging that sexual expression and sexual energy are inherently part of life and there's no way to separate them out from all that is.

Yes. This is what I've been saying all along, without hearing myself. Sexual energy is a part of the flow of life is a part of eating dinner is a part of doing the dishes is sitting on the sofa is walking on the beach and feeling the cold sand under the soles of your feet is orgasm is God is . . .

It's not that the sex part is all that special. We've just cordoned that part of ourselves off behind a red rope, all by itself. We vilify it, we worship it, when in fact it's simply who we are.

We might have a tendency—I might have a tendency—after a lifetime of believing deep down that my body and my desires are bad, to go to the other extreme and claim sex is everything! Sexual energy is supreme!

But that would be another distortion. Sexual energy is what it is. Part of being human. A strange and wonderful part of being alive.

13
building pleasure

We've learned how to receive pleasure and how to circulate that pleasure through our bodies. Now let's talk about allowing all that delicious pleasure to build!

When you're playing around with energy and sensation like we've been doing, it's only natural you might sometimes start to feel, well, aroused. It's possible none of this will feel sexual at all for you, but if you do find these practices are turning you on, I have a little challenge for you. Next time you want to have sex (with yourself or someone else), what if you pause? For a long time? That's right. What if you don't have sex? What will happen if—just this once—you choose *not* to climax? At least, not right away. Where will all that energy *go*? Why don't you try it and see? I don't mean cutting that feeling off or trying to submerge it. I mean: Can you be right here with it?

It's funny how the minute we feel desire, we want to offload it as fast as we can. You'd think we'd want to hold onto that scintillating feeling as long as possible, but it can be uncomfortable holding all that sensation within ourselves. The minute we feel the buildup of pleasure, we want to get rid of it. We can't handle the tension of our own wanting. Think about it. Don't we race to climax the same way we'd rush to put out a blazing fire? Why? Why do we do that?

"Um, Heather, we do it because it feels good."

Well, yeah, of course it does. But desire feels good too, right? And you know the minute you come, that desire's going to vanish—poof!

What would it feel like to sit with all that turn-on and wanting inside your body? What if, instead of racing to extinguish it, you . . . felt it? What if you allowed yourself to luxuriate in the decadence of your longing, just for a little while?

We've been conditioned to assume that arousal must lead to climax. That feeling of resolution is fantastic, but it's not the only experience you can have with your wanting. You can also sit with it. Or ride it. Let it flow through you, follow it and see where it leads. Allow whatever sensation is here to expand past the point where you'd normally surrender into orgasm.

Next time you feel those flurries of desire flicker within you, can you be curious? The same way you were curious while massaging your hand, the same way you were attentive to your enjoyment of food? Will it kill you to feel this?

practice: ride the wave

For this one, you'll want to wait for a time when you're feeling really turned on. If you're not feeling it right now, go ahead and keep reading. When the time is right, come back, pick this book up again and play.

Do you feel turned on? Good!

First of all, as always, take a breath.

In—and out.

If you are aroused, you're probably feeling some pressure and intensity in and around your wilderness. Breathe into that and just feel it. Smile into that feeling. Hi there!

Now see if you can feel some other part of your body too, at the same time. How about your foot? How's your foot feeling right now? Well, that's interesting. Your wilderness is raring to go, but I'll bet you anything your foot's just chilling. Maybe not.

Whatever's going on, pay attention. See if you can feel from your foot up into your shin, from your shin into your knee, your knee to your thigh, from your thigh into your hip socket.

Now see if you can feel the whole surface of your body at once.

There's a revelation, huh?

What about the interior of your body? Can you feel that? Can you feel your heart beating?

Even if you can't feel your whole body all at once, trust there's something here, something interesting. I promise you there is.

It's possible you may feel very uncomfortable.

You might start feeling like, oh my god, I'd really rather just come already. You can of course do that whenever you want.

But what if, instead of dumping your desire, you breathe deeply into it?

What if you ride what you're feeling like a wave?

Waves surge, then subside, again and again.

Is it possible this feeling is like that too?

Can you ride this sensation the same way you'd ride a wave on the ocean, in a little boat?

Or floating on your back, arms outstretched, your face to the sun.

Allow yourself to feel all of you.

Breathe your breath very gently up to your head.

Breathe it out into the palms of your hands.

Let that dense poignant gnawing in your pelvis spread out. Spread it around like cake batter, all through you. Down through your thighs, up through your belly. Let it disintegrate, let it sparkle, let it reconstitute into density, then dissipate again.

It could be that the desire vanishes. That's fine. As always, there's nothing for you to *do* here. No way to get this right or get it wrong. It's just you on your little boat on the ocean, riding the swells of the waves, breathing, smiling into your body, being gentle with yourself, seeing what's here.

Feel free to climax if that's what you want. But play with this off and on, and see if there isn't something nourishing in allowing the sensations inside of you to just *be*. Let that raw potent energy seep deep into the cells of your body, into your muscles, into the core of your bones.

How do you feel?

As you re-enter your daily life, do you feel quenched? Frustrated? Soothed? Perplexed?

April 2022

I've been toying lately with not climaxing. Not even touching myself at all. I have the will to do this now, because I am bored with self-pleasuring, bored with orgasm, bored, bored, bored. Finally—at last—I'm just barely bored enough to withstand the wanting and wait to see what's on the other side. Wow, it took a lot of years to get to this point! But finally I'm more curious what it will feel like if I don't come, what it will feel like if instead I run that libidinous current all through me.

A languorous quality starts to wind its way through my body. I love it. It's still no match for an orgasm, but like I said I'm bored with that so I'm willing to play around with this.

I breathe and breathe. This is a floating unfurling. Expansive beyond anything I've ever known. The pleasurable sensation is still there, strong enough that if I wanted, I could stop everything and go for the gold. But I don't want to stop this liquid evolution.

Bliss spills out my third eye, pours through all the cells of my body. Light comes out my fingers and toes and eyeballs. The air in my nostrils is exquisitely soft and cool as it travels through my throat, into my lungs. A delicate powerful pleasure fills me up and clears me out and extends me in all directions to every corner of the universe. I ground down into the energy of the earth, remembering to remain rooted. Sometimes it does feel like I could just float away, so grounding comforts me.

I'm in my own contentment, not needing the presence of anyone else. I am magnificent in my own vastness, the way the night sky is magnificent.

Giving myself over to the enormity of this energy reminds me of kayaking on the ocean—a little terrifying but also awe-inspiring. I can be so afraid of this immense power inside me, but in fact, I am of the ocean. I too am made of salt water. I can just be with the hugeness, riding the sunlit waves. Sometimes those waves are immense, sometimes they *slop and sloop. I can allow a big one to crash through me, allow myself to spill onto the shore, fizzing across the sand, then back out toward the horizon, back to the deep.*

Writing this now, in my fluffy pink bathrobe, drinking my coffee, I feel like plump fruit on the vine. My lips feel full. My legs are alive, my toes are alive. I feel fierce, but in a soft way.

Today I'll take these ocean waves with me. I'll feel them splashing up through my belly, through my nipples, my heart, sloshing around my throat. Nothing to hold onto. There was never anything to hold onto in the first place. It's time to know this: All is well. No. Matter. What.

14
performance anxiety

A strange anxiety's building in me as we approach the end of this book. I'm feeling shut down around the topic of sensuality, let alone sex. I feel this pressure to deliver something to you. The goods, I guess? Like I've got to dominate the page the way a model dominates the runway. I've got to demonstrate I know what I'm talking about. It's time to pull out all the stops and put on my one-woman Halftime Show for you, with fireworks.

But all I want to do is check out.

I know this feeling. This is that same pressure I'd feel years ago when I was about to have sex with someone, and I could see the whole thing laid out before me. I'd race to assess whether my body was capable of making it to the finish line. I could never seem to orgasm in a timely manner.

But the end goal of this book is not intercourse. It's not even better sex. Even when I do talk about sex, the goal is this: Allow any thought of a goal to evaporate and move from there. Still, it feels like these pages are driving toward some soaring finale! And that's precisely what kills my desire to keep going. So I have to keep reminding myself this isn't a performance.

The other day I was watching this show with Honey Pie (Ex #1), and I literally jumped up off the sofa during one of the sex scenes. The main character in the show falls for a guy at her work. In one scene, she and her husband are having what should be great sex—she's wearing a black lace confection, cooing how much she wants him as he looms over her, rugged and bare-chested. But the whole thing feels forced. Later she has sex with the guy she's super into, and it's silent, fumbling, almost uninteresting except for the look in her eyes as she meets his.

That's when I jumped off the sofa. I was like, *"That's* real! That's real sex! That's what I'm talking about!" Honey Pie rolled his eyes and smiled, then got up to get more snacks.

Yeah, watching TV with me can be annoying. I've always got a running commentary going about any sex that's happening. "Look at that! I guarantee you there's no pleasure happening there. There's no way she's coming like that."

It's not that that first scene couldn't have been electric, but for me, phenomenal sex happens *within and between* the bodies and souls involved. If nothing's going on there, it doesn't matter how hot the scene looks. It's just a big fizzle.

We've got a lot of unexamined assumptions in this culture about what it means to be sexual or to "have sex." Our assumptions are deeply rooted in (among other things) a mindset that tells us what matters in life is first survival and after that, achievement and the endless attainment of various goals. Yes, I'm talking about capitalism. This orientation to the world is so ingrained, it infiltrates every facet of our existence until we've come to think of even ourselves and others as objects or commodities. I know you know this. So even a relationship or a sexual experience becomes one more thing to acquire, so we can cross it off our bucket list. But there is a different paradigm for what it means to be alive and in communion with others. That's to just be here.

Did you take a breath just now? Good!

I'm telling you, if you go at this whole thing with the idea there's some mountain to scale, some ultimate sexual or spiritual experience just around the corner, you will be—ultimately—disappointed. Any peak experience is by definition transcendent. It's lifting you up above the realm of the ordinary. That's great, but at some point you have to come back down off the mountain. If your focus is always on the next mountain, you're missing what's happening right now.

practice: go slow

I can only speak from personal experience on this one, so I'm talking to those of you with pussies here.

If you too feel pressure to climax, here's what I suggest:

Slow. Down.

Way, way, way, way down.

You've got to find a partner who understands (or teach the one you've got) just how long it takes your body to become fully aroused. And I'm talking wet, engorged, begging-for-sex aroused. Even then, it could take even more time than that for you to relax into orgasm. For some of us, it can take much longer than we've been told is normal. Give yourself a *ton* of time. Oh yeah, and don't assume old fashioned intercourse alone is going to do it for you. That does *not* work for women—are you sitting down—70% of the time. If you don't believe me, check out the Kinsey Institute's article *How Often Do Women Orgasm During Sex?*

February 2023

People keep asking when I'm going to date again. The question makes me uncomfortable, because it implies I'm on some deadline I never agreed to. It also makes me feel like something's wrong with me, like I'm not a whole person if I'm not with another person.

People assume if I like sex so much, I must want to have it all the time. They think I'm some super-turned-on-down-for-anything sex maven. I'm so not. For the most part I need to take things super slow. Ideally, if I'm having sex with someone, I'm in love with them. At the very least, I've got to feel a deep affection. Otherwise it sucks. I just learned there's a name for this: demisexuality. Who knew?

I'm not interested in trying to force anything now, whether it's some erotic tryst or a new relationship. My sexual energy is mysterious. It doesn't run on a timeline. It doesn't act like it should or come on demand. It does not respond well to expectations. It's mercurial, here one second and gone the next. I can't will myself to feel sensual. In fact, the more I try, the more that elusive feeling slips away.

February 2022

I'm watching these videos that teach you how to open up the chakras through various sexual poses, as in how to reach next-level epic sacred connected sex.

And I have completely. Shut. Down. I feel so intimidated. I've watched all these videos, and now I just want to run away, go to sleep, or watch TV.

I've wanted to learn this for so long, ever since I saw those sloooow sex scenes in The Last Mistress and in Lust, Caution. What was that? It wasn't like sex I'd seen in any other movie. Those scenes still haunt me. How does one get to the place of having that kind of transcendent experience?

Well, now I know, and I'm completely shut down. It looks like it's so much work and riddled with landmines. What if something hurts? What if you don't fit together right? What if I'm not strong enough? (I'm sorry—me on top in plank pose? Um, no). How on earth am I going to orgasm in these postures? I know climax isn't the point here, but how's this even going to feel good?

God help me, I can't see myself doing half these positions with any kind of ease or enjoyment. Give me some interstellar lover with magical powers. Maybe he could pull it off, with me in tow. But me? Doing this with a normal human being? I'm exhausted just thinking about it.

How will I find a partner who either A. knows how to do this (in which case won't I be jealous of who he did it with before?) or B. doesn't know how to do this but is willing to learn (so we'll be two newbies going at it, and we'll default back to plain old fucking)?

I don't know that further study is the solution for me. I can't get a handle on anything to do with technique. Reading a sex manual is like reading a war history. I can read and reread it, but I can't retain the information or even keep track of all the bullet points.

I have to get over this. It's just like yoga. I love the stretching exercises and hate everything that requires effort. I need to push past doing what comes easy for me.

I hope I find a partner sometime in the not-so-distant future who I can continue this journey with. That said, every time someone asks if I'm ready to date again, the answer is No! As in, are you kidding? Yeah, no. For now there's plenty to explore on my own.

15
s-e-x

Kissing's the best.
Lips locked in lightly. Tongues slapping into each other. Juicy kisses.
Fresh, urgent, tender kisses.
Kisses are the very best.
Kisses that invite, kisses that tease, kisses that request. Kisses getting to know you better. Kisses telling you what I'm thinking. Kisses that love love love you all over. Kisses asking a question, telling volumes, telling secrets. Kisses that haunt you. Need you. Kisses that worship and adore and inspire. Kisses that deliver.
Oh, the kisses!
Kisses beseeching. Kisses commanding. Kisses bestowing.
Confirming.
Affirming.
Peck.
Pluck.
Fuck.
Oh yes, now we fuck.

———

So, to be clear. Nothing you learn from this book needs to lead to sex. Ever. You could cultivate your sexual energy till the cows come home. You could bliss out on all these sensations in your body, this interplay between you and the universe—forever—and that would be a fabulous existence. However, if you want to take this taste of ambrosia you're discovering and share it with someone else, by all means do it!

I started out this chapter with my brainstorm on kisses, because, well, kisses are so easy. They're so fun. At the same time, a powerful kiss can cut you to the quick. Great sex is like that. It can be fun, easy, connected. It can be dark and dangerous and weird. It can be anything, really. For so many of us though, sex (unlike kisses) has got all bungled up. We have so many expectations and issues; there's so much at stake. Whether we're with a new partner or in a long-term relationship, we bring so much baggage to bed with us.

Ever since I started writing about sex, people talk to me like they're going to confession. I can't count the times someone's said to me, "You're the only person I can talk to about this." Why is that? Why can't we be more vulnerable with each other? We'd all be so much better off if we would talk to each other about this stuff. And I mean, what's really going on with us sexually. Because I'll tell you what. People aren't coming up to me saying, "Oh, I'm having the best sex of my life. I'm just such a maniac in bed." Okay, well, some people do say that, but they are definitely in the minority! No, we all —all of us, as far as I can tell—have our issues when it comes to sex. Seriously though, most of us are not that great at it. How could we be? Nobody teaches us any of this. It's not something we're taught to make a priority.

We're exhausted, for one thing. We're given a million reasons to judge our bodies and our fantasies and our desires. Or our lack of desire! Whatever it is we're experiencing, we think it should be different. It should be dirtier. It should be more heart-centered. We shouldn't want what we want, we should want what we don't want.

Let me be the first to say it. I love, love, love sex. And sometimes, I am not the greatest lover. At all. Sometimes I am. But sometimes, seriously, I'm not.

I'm not going to give you a practice for this chapter. What are you going do, hold this book over your partner's head while you're going at it? (I've, um, done that. I kept losing my place. Like I said, not always the greatest lover).

Can we all be gentle with ourselves, get educated and get naked and play around and see what happens?

What I hope you're learning here is to *be present with yourself*, to attend to yourself, especially when you're having sex. Everything we've been practicing—the breathing, tuning in to our bodies, the circulation of sensation and pleasure—can open you up to a truly exquisite experience of sex with another person if that's something you want.

It all seemed so mundane, right? All that breathing. But here we are. You've got some sparkle in you. You can feel into the flow of life. Bring this sense of presence with you to your nakedness, bring it into an embrace with your lover, bring it into wild lovemaking, bring it into each and every moment of your existence.

Okay, that's a lot. You know what I mean. Do your best.

practice: the goal is no goal

I said I wasn't going to give you a practice for this chapter, and in a way that's true. I mean, the name of this one says it all.

Just like you did with building pleasure in yourself, it can be a treat to approach partnered sex (and solo sex) with no goal of orgasm. Just being with the sensations in your body, whatever they may be. Allowing them to surface in you and fade away like those waves on the ocean. Letting them build and subside and build again.

Give yourself/yourselves a bunch of time. Agree you're going to go through the motions of starting to have sex, but with no timeline whatsoever. No goal of climax. No goal of anything at all.

You can turn on some soothing music, if you want. Emphasis on the word "soothing."

I suppose you could set a timer—for like, at least an hour—but only if the thought of this vast swathe of unstructured time makes you anxious.

Sensual massage can be a good place to start. Or going down on each other. Both of these will give you room for extended leisurely play.

You might fall asleep, then wake up, then start again.

What about penetration? With no goal?? Sure, why not. Try it out and see, if that's what you feel like doing. Or not.

Allow yourself for once in your life to feel what you're feeling (or not feeling). Be honest with yourself. What's here? Right this second? And now? Pleasure doesn't always move in a straight line. It plays hide and seek. It comes and goes, rises and falls, disappears and returns. Allow it to be what it is. However much or little you feel is 100% okay.

Breathe. Breathe together. Long, deep, slow breaths. Oh yes, remember to breathe and breathe and breathe.

Have fun! Laugh at how boring and ludicrous it is to roll around together doing absolutely nothing at all.

A heads up: If you do this no-goal thing long enough, you may very well wind up climaxing. But don't think about that! Just enjoy. And again, if you don't, that's fine because the whole goal is NO GOAL. Seriously. If you get to the end of this process and you haven't had whatever you think of as S-E-X, notice if that feels like a failure to you. How could that be a failure? The goal was no goal! How does your body feel? How do you feel in your soul? As always, be curious. And kind.

If you enjoyed this practice, you might want to check out the history of *karezza*, a method developed in the late 1800s by Dr. Alice Bunker Stockham, an American Quaker. It's a different practice from this but there are similarities.

I know this isn't the most exciting thing you've ever tried, but that's not the point. And playing with this doesn't mean sex will never be conventional again or kinky or whatever it is that floats your boat. Of course it will. But what's the point of kink if you're not fully in your body? Why not do yourself a favor and establish a new baseline of sensation? How much more intense will it be when you can inhabit with the full force of your being whatever you and your partner concoct together next?

Okay, that's it. I'm not punching above my class here. If you want to have better sex, go find a good sex educator. And check out my resources page at heatherleannechapman.com.

February 2023
I had sex again.
After two years.
Wow.
It was hot. It was fun. Strange. I mean, yes, it had been two years, but I hadn't had sex with someone who's not my committed partner in nearly five years. So yeah, strange. Enlightening.

I could write and write about that day, that fantastic meal. His grin. That grin's gotten me in a lot of trouble. Our flirtation was vibrant and alive, a tantalizing build-up, the wondering if this might happen—oh, we both just admitted we want this to happen—okay, when is it happening?

I drove home. There was an escalation of texts. I drove back. The minute I arrived I realized I'd washed off all my makeup and was wearing a dumpy bra. These aren't things I've thought about in forever.

But there was no racing through my brain to determine whether I was ready for this. I'd already checked in with myself before I replied "Yes," before I even left the house. I was ready. My body was ready, and what I mean by that is I was warm, loose, easy. Feeling like an airplane anticipating liftoff.

The preciousness of kisses and the feel of his mouth against mine—also weird after no kisses for so very long. And because, well, we'd kissed a long time ago, when we were different people. Different yet exactly the same. I knew him. I knew the feel of his face.

There was a warmth and a rootedness to us. I felt very much in my own skin and at the same time fully aware of the feel of his skin on mine. I felt him shudder as I dragged my hands up and down his back. It was a big deal for me to have sex after all this time. And yes, my whole body was lit up and wanting him, so everything cascaded in a perfect unfolding.

I caught myself performing for him, wanting to impress him. The fastness of it all intimidated me. Oh, I was down for it, but I'm accustomed now to a 12-course meal, taking my *time and reveling in each sensation. Packing all that into a sudden fuck was a challenge.*

At the same time, I was able to drop fully into my body. I was able to ride the waves of sensation, to enjoy the deliciousness of it all, to revel in my own wanting of him, as much as in his wanting of me.

*I was with myself.
The whole time, I was with myself.
This was the thing afterwards I was most happy about. I didn't abandon myself. I was right there, every second.*

That moment our eyes met, that's the moment. A recognition that startles you at your core.

In the morning we had a good conversation over coffee. He walked me out to my car in the early dawn. And. Life goes on. At this point in my life, sex is both welcome and celebrated, and it's not the only thing in my world. Surprise! Even though I'm writing a book about it! No, it's not even remotely the only thing in my world.

I don't know if we'll do this again. It's likely we will. It was really fun. And, I want more. We each want so much more in different ways. I was never able to explain it to him then and don't seem to be able to convey it now—this longing I have for a whole-body ultra-sensory experience. An experience of pleasure and connection beyond orgasm. Whatever it is I still haven't known, that's what I want to know now with another person, ideally someone I love.

So, yeah. That happened.

16
you are enough

YOU WAIT FOR A DOOR TO OPEN.
BUT THE DOOR IS OPEN.
YOU ARE HERE.

CAN YOU REST?
CAN YOU PLEASE, PLEASE, PLEASE, PLEASE REST?
SINK INTO YOUR BONES.
LET THE EVENING'S TWILIGHT ENTER YOU.

TOUCH THIS MOMENT, AND YOU TOUCH ALL THINGS.
LAND WITHIN YOURSELF, AND ALL WORLDS COLLIDE WITHIN YOU.

YOU ARE LOVE, WE ARE LOVE, IT IS ALL, YES, LOVE.

———

What I'm going to say now is so important I wanted to put it at the beginning of this book, but I knew you wouldn't listen to me. I mean, I wouldn't listen, if I were you. So, can we sit down for a second? Can I say something to you? There's something you've got to do if you want to feel more fully alive in your body.

You've got to slow down.

Seriously.

Nothing here will do you any good if you're so burned out you can't feel anything. Slowing down and resting are key to the whole process. You must rest.

I won't go on and on about this. We all know how insane the pressure is to go go go. So, just stop already.

practice: get some sleep

I heard about this practice on Gretchen Rubin's podcast, and I think it's brilliant.

Pick up your phone and set an alarm. Not to wake up, but to go to bed. What time do you need to get to sleep so you wake up refreshed? Set your alarm for 30 minutes before that, and set it to repeat every night.

When the timer goes off, stop what you're doing and get ready for bed. If this is the only thing you do in this whole book, you will be on your way to crashing into that wild elephant life force energy of yours.

practice: stay in bed

This one comes with a caveat. If you have a baby or small children and you don't know one single person who can watch them for four hours one day of your life, ignore this practice and skip ahead. If that's not you though, keep reading!

Look at your calendar and find one free morning this month.

Oh, I'm sorry, you don't have a free morning this month? Cancel something.

Block out the whole morning with this calendar item: STAY IN BED.

Now, do it!

I don't care what you do that morning as long as you stay in that bed! Okay, maybe get up first and make yourself a plate of french toast, but then go right back and eat it in bed. Watch old movies. Read a book. Call a friend. Sleep. Whatever.

I don't want to hear why you don't have time to do this. You have time to do this.

This is a little trick of mine. It's the #1 thing I do to boost my productivity, and let me tell you, I am a very productive, crazy-organized person. The thing is, once I give myself this kind of time, and then I finally do get out of bed, I'm ready to take on the world. But you have to really do it. You have to stay in that bed.

Did you do the last two practices?

Go back and do them!

I don't want to talk to you until you've got enough sleep and you've stayed in bed one whole morning.

Okay, did you do it now?

I'll know if you did, because you'll have this fresh glow, and you'll give me this look like, "Oh wow, Heather, what just happened to me?"

You're welcome.

Like I've been trying to tell you, I know some stuff.

Now, I can't be following you around reminding you to rest. This is on you. And this isn't a one-time thing. It needs to be an all-the-time thing. It can be as simple as pausing to drink a glass of water, but all the ancient secrets in the world won't do you any good if you're just plain exhausted.

I know you don't have the time for this. I know. I do know this world we live in.

But you know what? I take that back. As much as the world drives us, we drive ourselves just as much, if not more. If you don't have the time, then make it.

Make. Time.

You do it all the time.

You make time all the time for everybody else.

Don't you? You do.

You just don't make time for you.

The real issue here is you don't believe YOU *deserve* the time.

Oh.

Well, that gets down to it.

Is this why you put everyone else first?

Is this why you kill yourself with work?

Is this why you can't take even five minutes to sit down?

This is big.

You see, I can tell you how to feel amazing in your body, but what good is that going to do you if you don't think you deserve to feel amazing? If you think you're unworthy of feeling that good?

Remember that thing I told you to write down before? You thought it was silly, didn't you?

I am worthy of feeling good.

Somehow, you've got it in your head that you're not enough. You've got all kinds of ways of covering that up. Putting everybody else first. Working, taking care of, building, creating—you know, doing things. That's all great. But what about you?

Here's the question:

Do you feel like you're enough?

Just as you are.

If you never did another thing the rest of your life, did you do enough?

Are you enough?

Okay, maybe this is painful.

Why don't you stop and feel whatever that is you're feeling for a second.

I'd like to share with you what I know:

You are enough.

Exactly as you are, you are enough.

You always were enough, you'll always be enough, and there's nothing you can do or say or achieve that has any impact on that whatsoever.

You exist! You're a part of this Universe! No less than a ray of sunshine or a baby rabbit. I guess that's a bunny. No less than a fuzzy baby bunny! Sink into that. See if you can feel that in your bones, that kind of worthiness.

You don't need to prove your right to exist on this planet. You're already here! In all honesty, nobody's keeping score anyway. Oh sure, maybe your neighbors are, or maybe your family is, but deep down do you really care about that game? Do you? What if you just dropped the ball for once and stopped? You might be surprised. The Universe might rush up and give you a giant sloppy kiss on the cheek. It might take you by the hand and say, *Oh, finally! There's something I've been wanting to show you, but you're always so busy! Come see!*

You don't even have to believe you're deserving in order to make time for yourself. You can take one outrageous action after another, whether or not you think you're worthy, whether or not you have the time. Here's a radical idea: Take a nap. If you're someone who always holds it, let yourself go pee.

We're always and forever pushing that boulder up the hill, but resting is part of the ebb and flow of life. If we don't ebb, we can't flow. What I suggest now is you take a deep breath and surrender to what is. Just for this one second, there's nothing for you to do. Let this be an *un*doing. Let yourself be undone, just for this moment.

Over time this question of whether or not you're worthy or deserving or enough may very well become irrelevant. The practice of being kind to yourself will reshape you into a vessel that can withstand more and more the unbearable wonder of being alive.

———

May 2018

I am perpetually forcing my body to do things it doesn't want to do—checking things off of lists, basically. Getting shit done.

And I get a lot of goodies for this kind of behavior. This part of me gets so much approval from our society, but I happen to know it's a deeply unhealthy part of me.

When I asked my pussy how she felt this morning, I felt a yearning reaching up and out of that part of myself. Like a voice that's been locked up for so very long and suddenly in this moment it realizes I am listening and it's pleading with me to stop and hear it. And all it wants is to go outside, to lie in the grass, to lie on the beach, to be in the water, to be in the woods. That is all it wants. And it says to me the reason it wants it is that that is all that matters. Life is so short. That is all that matters.

17
closing

UNDER THE SURFACE OF THIS MOMENT LIES
BLISS
CAN YOU FEEL ITS BUBBLES SURFACE BENEATH YOUR VENEER?
THE GOLD EXUDING FROM INSIDE YOU?
FIREFLIES FLITTING IN AND ABOUT THE CAVITY OF YOUR HEART
YOU ARE WIDE OPEN
YOU ARE
STARLIGHT
YOU ARE MAGIC ENCAPSULATED IN A HUMAN BODY
YOU DON'T EVEN KNOW IT
DO YOU?

March 2022

Last night I thought to myself: Why am I always trying to get people into their bodies? What's so great about the body? We're all going to die anyway. These are just bags of skin we're all walking around in. Doomed to fail. Guaranteed to return to the ground one way or another. Why do I care so much about being in my body? It won't last. Shouldn't I focus instead on my spirit, my soul, that which is eternal?

But this body is all I've got. As long as I'm alive, this is the apparatus through which I'll experience my entire existence. Whether I'm tuned in or not will have a massive impact on the quality of every one of my days. I can live a numinous life, or I can live in a state of chronic disconnect.

This moment is all there is. At least, it's what I've got access to. Let me fill this with presence, with wonder. While I'm here, let me really be here.

Oh wow, as I was thinking: What's this all about anyway? Why are we here? I looked up, and way beyond the branches of a big tree I saw a tiny speck of a hummingbird darting around up there in the blue. And what is this life to the hummingbird? Does it even ask why it's here? What's the purpose of all this? I highly doubt it. I'm pretty sure it's just enjoying the warmth of the morning sun on its back. I'm pretty sure it's like, Fuck, I love to fly! I can see everything! I can go anywhere! This is so fun! Where's my next flower?

I know I can get overly enthusiastic. There's a good chance you're not feeling like a happy little hummingbird right now. I know how tough it can be to get through a day, let alone enjoy it. Sometimes—hell, most of the time—the last thing you want to think about is your vitality, because, well, you don't have any. Maybe you suffer from chronic pain. Maybe the momentum of fatigue or inertia is too much for you to overcome right now. Or you can't seem to stop working so hard. Maybe you keep submerging your wants and desires to accommodate the ones you love. Or you're just more comfortable plowing through life a little unconscious.

Go ahead and sit on that sofa as long as you need. It's totally fine. Here's the thing. One day, you're going to remember this book. You're going to take a breath in, and you're going to be like, oh yeah.

That.

In—and out.

When that moment occurs, I'd like you to remember the invitation that's always here for you, always and forever in each second of your life. The invitation to arrive. Here. Just as you are. To *be* here. And then to let yourself feel a little bit more.

January 2023
A disturbing thing is happening. As I barrel toward the completion of this book, my body has shut down. I don't know why this is such a surprise. My physical activity has dropped to next to nothing, and from there, one thing's led to another, so now my body feels like a big lump. I feel sludgy and dull and dead. Sex is the last thing on my mind, except I'm writing this book, and so sex hangs over me as something I should be interested in but in fact could care less about at the moment.

I feel like a sloth. I don't want to do anything. The more I sink into this blah feeling, the harder it is to escape. It becomes, simply, my existence. A dull plodding through the minutes of my day. Doing this task, doing that. Even when I come back to my breath or the feeling tone in my body, nothing interesting happens.

I'm so tired. If I could sleep and sleep and sleep, it still wouldn't be enough sleep.

Here I am, cheerleading people to Be in your body! Feel what you're feeling! But right now I'm cheerleading from a bench on the sidelines.

I clutch at these pages like a drowning person—these pages I wrote myself. I reread them with a desperation that propels me forward one page, one half-hearted inhale at a time.

And? It's working.

This morning I woke up and lurched to my meditation cushion. Thirty minutes of bringing my attention back to this moment, back to this breath. Then I danced for the first time in a long time. It felt so good. Through dance I discovered myself again as the erotic being I am. I keep thinking I've turned into a slug, but that's not true.

I forced myself to read through these last chapters. Where I chide you to get up on your feet and do the Five Gates breathing exercise, I did it myself. I stood up. I breathed earth energy in through my feet, and yes, my body did feel more alive.

Then I woke up at 5 am. There it was again! That deep, primal hunger within me. I'm back! I'm still here! I'm still alive in the most potent way.

That spark, that hunger—it comes and goes. Who knows what draws it forward. Hormones? Attention? Attraction? Love?

Anyway, I danced some more. I wrote some more. And here I am back at the intersection of me and divine inspiration.

We've covered a lot of ground here. There's a lot to remember! Oh, but it's not so much. You can refer to the Contents page at the beginning of the book to find each of the practices we've tried out. Here's a recap:

Breathe. This one's easy. You've got the hang of this. Just remember to breathe *all* the way down into your wilderness, your beautiful, yummy, lovable sexual organs. That's the part no one tells you, the magic part.

Say hi to your wilderness. *Hi there. How are you?* Listen. Feel. Connect up first thing when you wake up. Remember, this isn't about feeling turned on all the time. It's about landing in your center, feeling authentic and whole. Tap into this sacred power source every single day. Cultivate a sense of shameless innocence and unabashed joy towards your own body.

Play around with orbiting. Imagine golden oil flowing through you as it traces an egg-like path through your body. From the top of your head, down your spine, all the way down to your legs and feet. Then breathe in that gold sparkle right up the front of your body. Tap into the feeling of this current of life that's always flowing through you.

Move your body. Stretch. Do a little dance, even just for five minutes! Bounce, shake. Go outside, go for a walk. Notice the feeling tone in your body. Accept any tension that's there and see if you can melt around it.

Touch yourself. Hug yourself. Give your breasts some love. Hello beauties! Slather them up in the shower and give your nipples a pinch. *Smile* into them. Beam love into them and any other part of your body that needs it. Massage your hands. Rub your neck. When you've got a minute, grab some oil and anoint yourself.

Be kind to yourself. Make space for whatever it is you're feeling right now. Allow whatever shame or trauma is surfacing to just be here. Reach out to someone you trust if you need support. Learn to practice consent with yourself.

Receive pleasure. Notice things you appreciate during your day and get in there and relish them. Eat with gusto. Pay attention to the flavors and textures in that very first bite of food. Chew each bite eleven times to get yourself to slow down. Savor the smell and taste of your morning coffee. Revel in the banquet of life laid out for you every single day.

Circulate pleasure. Breathe as you circulate shimmering sensation all through your body. Breathe in the energy of the earth, the air, all of life. Experiment with the different flavors of feeling you can run through your body. Imagine the breath is your lover, whispering through you.

Build pleasure. Play with postponing your orgasm. Savor that carnal wanting in your body and just be with the tension of your desire. Ride the wave, as it pulsates through you. Let that potent energy feed and nourish all the cells of your body.

Go slow. Remember there's no landing to nail here. Nothing to achieve. Keep bringing your attention back to what's happening inside you right now. Take your time. Take as much time as *you* need. Let yourself be with yourself, at last.

Play. Have fun! Play around with what it feels like to commune with someone else without any goal or destination in mind. Be intimate not only with your lover but also with yourself.

Rest. Get some sleep, will you?! Every now and then, stay in bed for one whole morning. Add it to your calendar to do absolutely nothing. Drink some water.

practice: soap bubbles

Sit and breathe.

Picture soap bubbles rising out of the top of your head

Emerging from the surface of your skin, from all over your body

Little soap bubbles

Catching the light

Bouncing, gleaming, floating, drifting

Popping ever so delicately

Pop, pop, pop

Little soap bubbles up from your tailbone, up through your sternum, up through your heart, through your neck, through your brain, up through the blowhole in the top of your head.

You're a human bubble machine! Blowing soap bubbles out the top of your head! How fantastic! How delightful. How cheerful. Go, little soap bubbles, go.

Rise and pop, rise and pop.

Soap bubbles!

Exiting your body in all directions

Emerging from the core of you, out your cells, out the surface of your skin, all over your body

Bye, bye little bubbles, bye, bye

Pop, pop, pop

Oh no! We're at end of the last chapter, which means you and I have to say goodbye.

My heart feels so large right now. I'm tearing up.

I'll miss you!

I'll miss so much these conversations where I talk and you listen!

Of course, you can always reach out and find me.

But for now, this is where we part ways.

You have changed me, truly. You, who called forth from me all these words. So, thank you. It was all for you, remember? Our pinky-finger pact. Stay the course. Come back again and again to the endeavor of opening to this life.

Despite telling you not to focus on a goal, my quest continues to experience the ever-elusive supernatural bliss of tantric sex! I'll keep you posted on that one. Not having a committed partner is a major obstacle at the moment. Probably for the best. I'd never have completed this book if I'd been levitating with my hot tantric lover all day. So, let's both be thankful for all this alone time I've had, shall we? It's been beneficial for us both.

What *are* we doing here anyway? On this planet? Who knows. Because of you I've dove deeper into that question than I've ever done before. There's still no answer for me, but the question prods me to be more fully here. In it. To sink down into this moment and feel the air in my nostrils, hear the burble of the river, to wipe these tears from my face and marvel at the sensuousness of wetness on skin.

Looking back at this brief time together, what's it been about? I invited you into something. What was it? Can you remember? Did you even fully understand what it was to begin with?

Doesn't matter. And you know why? Because the invitation is always right here. It's a standing invitation. It's always new and fresh, particular to this moment. It's always here for you, but never the same, and it's never what you thought it was going to be. It's whatever is here right now. Within you. You just have to remember. The universe isn't going to get in your face and tell you, *Hey! Remember to breathe! Remember to feel your wilderness!* In the end you're the one returning yourself day after day into a deeper and sweeter experience of this strange and wonderful life.

You are more vast and powerful than you know. The sexual spark within you is one path you can follow into the mystery within. There are infinite other paths, but what we've been playing with here—cultivating sexual energy and the practice of deep sensual embodiment—this is the trail I've done my best to light up for you.

This radiant presence is your birthright as a living creature on this planet. Who knows why, but isn't it great? Yes, our lives may be filled with drudgery, injustice, chaos, and pain, but they're filled with this too.

Remember to breathe. Ground down into the earth, unfurl your tree roots deep down to the center of the earth. Let the sparkle of life flow through your limbs. Remember, above all, to be kind to yourself. Love every inch of you.

Okay, enough.

We're at the end.

This is that awkward goodbye where one person keeps gushing on and on, hugging you, and you're like, "Okay, byeeee."

Yeah, yeah, get on with your day! Maybe one day we'll meet in person and I'll tell you where I'm at on my journey and you can tell me all about yours.

I can't wait.

———

SHHHHHH
LISTEN
DO YOU HEAR THE TENDER SILENCE OF LIFE ENCIRCLING YOU?
YOU ARE OF THIS
DROP IN
DROP DOWN
BREATHE

BREATHE AND BREATHE AND BREATHE
BREATHE YOUR WAY INTO PRESENCE
INTO PLEASURE
BREATHE YOUR WAY INTO COMMUNION WITH ALL THAT IS
ALLOW YOUR HEART TO BE SQUEEZED BY A SWEETNESS YOU DO NOT COMPREHEND.
THERE IS ONLY THIS
AND THIS IS ENOUGH.
WILL YOU
TOUCH THIS?
WILL YOU
ENTER THIS?
THE EXTENSION OF THIS MOMENT, THROUGH YOUR PRESENCE
ALLOW IT TO UNFOLD
TASTE THE ANCIENT NECTAR DEEP WITHIN
SET FIRE TO THAT WHICH LIGHTS YOU FROM THE INSIDE
ONCE AND FOR ALL
ENCOUNTER THE WELLSPRING OF VITALITY
RADIANT SOURCE OF ALL THAT IS
WITHIN YOU.

about the author

Heather Leanne Chapman is a writer, mystic, and lifelong learner. For the past nine years, she's studied the art of pleasure, receiving, and whole-body aliveness.

In her previous lives she wrote two blogs: *You are Fed* (about food) and *How to Come Back to Life: my erotic project and return to self love* (about sex).

The Elixir Within is her first book.

To receive a download of a free guided practice from *The Elixir Within* recorded by the author, visit
www.heatherleannechapman.com/theelixirwithin

For information on workshops, contact Heather at
www.heatherleannechapman.com